Raising
Abel

Raising Abel

The Recovery of the Eschatological Imagination

JAMES ALISON

A Herder & Herder Book
The Crossroad Publishing Company
New York

The Crossroad Publishing Company
16 Penn Plaza, 481 Eighth Avenue
New York, NY 10001

Printed in the United States of America

Library of Congress Cataloging-in-Publication Data

Alison, James, 1959-
    Raising Abel : the recovery of the eschatological imagination / James
Alison.
        p.   cm.
    "A Crossroad Herder book."
    Includes bibliographical references and index.
    ISBN 0-8245-1565-X (pbk.)
    1. Eschatology. 2. Bible–Criticism, interpretation, etc.
3. Eschatology–Biblical teaching. 4. Jesus Christ–Crucifixion.
5. Jesus Christ–Resurrection. 6. Violence in the Bible.
7. Violence–Religious aspects–Christianity. 8. Sacrifice in the
Bible. 9. Girard, René, 1923-   . I. Title.
BT821.2.A45 1996
230–dc20   96-10684
                                                                  CIP

"Fix your minds on the things that are above..."

Contents

Preface

Some works of theology are informative, exploring what is to be believed for those in search of theological education who have insufficient facts at their disposal. This can often be profoundly helpful, as when someone discovers that what is really believed by the Church is quite different from what they had thought, and that there are councils and authorities to prove it. The present work has a slightly different approach, one which I would hope to prove therapeutic rather than informative. It takes for granted that, whether a believer or not, the reader, by virtue of being an educated part of Western society, comes already pre-soaked in a series of underlying attitudinal patterns formed by a discourse about "The End," "Hell," "Judgment," and "Heaven." It seems to me that we all have work to do to move beyond some of those attitudes, particularly in the last few years of the second millennium, where a strong recrudescence of apocalyptic language and sentiment is clearly in the air. It seems to me that the job of the Catholic theologian is, rather unapologetically, both to maintain the truth of what is believed for the benefit of believers, and to offer the possibility of something approaching sanity for those with no adherence to a formal structure of belief, who yet find themselves bewildered by a strident cacophony of voices advocating their allegiance to One who is to come.

In the pages that follow I have gone light on the mass of footnotes which often accompany academic theology. Because of this I may unwittingly give the impression that this is "all my own work." That would not be fair to the many people who have helped me and to the many well-camouflaged sources on which I have drawn. I would therefore like here to express some of my gratitude and acknowledgments: I owe a great debt to João Batista Libânio, S.J., whose course on Eschatology at the Jesuit Center of Studies in Belo Horizonte, Brazil, first brought home to me the importance of this field. I'm also deeply indebted to the homilies and the teaching of the New Testament of Timothy Radcliffe, O.P., during his period as prior of

Blackfriars, Oxford, as well as his essay " 'The Coming of the Son of Man': Mark's Gospel and the Subversion of the 'Apocalyptic Imagination' " in B. Davies, ed., *Language, Meaning and Love: Essays in Honour of Herbert McCabe* (London: Chapman, 1987). This essay has been an abiding source of stimulation and insight for me. I would have very much less understanding of Jesus of Nazareth and his world than I do had I not had access to the teaching and friendship of J. Duncan M. Derrett, whose exegetical studies are in a class of their own as regards insight and provocation. I would also like to acknowledge my several debts to Robert Hamerton-Kelly where these are not already footnoted.

My own understanding of many of the central facets of eschatology would never have got beyond the infantile had it not been for the grandeur of Joseph Ratzinger's book *Eschatology: Death and Eternal life* (Washington, D.C.: Catholic University of America Press, 1988). This is still the book I would unhesitatingly press into the hand of anyone wanting a more formal study of what the Church believes in matters eschatological. The two elegant volumes by Andrés Tornos, S.J., entitled *Escatología I & II* (Madrid: UPCM, 1989–1992), provide the best treatment I know of Christian hope and how to ask ourselves about history. It was the essay on the Ascension by Christoph von Schönborn, O.P., in his collection *La vie éternelle* (Paris: Seuil, 1994) which opened up to me the importance of that moment. Also in the field of theology I would like to mention the work of John Milbank, particularly a brilliant, and little-commented article in *Modern Theology* (7, no. 4 July 1991) entitled "The Name of Jesus: Incarnation, Atonement, Ecclesiology." This, as well as his ground-breaking contribution in the chapter of *Theology and Social Science* (Oxford: Blackwell, 1990) called "Founding the Supernatural," have been major sources of food, semi-digested in the ruminations which follow. The depth of my debt to the thought of René Girard is patent to all who know anything of that thought. Less evident, but of great value has been the thought of Jean-Michel Oughourlian, particularly as to the relationship between psychology, time, and memory, which I explore in chapter 5. His work *The Puppet of Desire* (Stanford, Calif.: Stanford University Press, 1991) opens significant new vistas in these and other areas. I was fortunate enough to receive a copy of Cesáreo Bandera's *The Sacred Game: The Genesis of Modern Literary Fiction* (University Park, Pa.: Penn State University Press, 1994) while preparing these pages, and would be honored to think that

Cesáreo might recognize the paternity of some of the brighter ideas in chapter 6.

This book is the author's translation and adaptation of a course that first saw the light of day as *Fijen las mentes en las cosas de arriba: recuperando la imaginación escatológica*. This course was given at the Instituto Pedro de Córdoba in Santiago de Chile in the second semester of 1994. The institute is a postgraduate center founded and run by the Dominican order. It is dedicated to the interdisciplinary study of the social realities of the Latin American countries, with particular emphasis on the interface between the social sciences and theology. Its pupils are drawn from a wide variety of different countries, lay people, female and male religious, and priests. Thus the immediate context of my attempt to rework some elements of the treatise on eschatology was the urgent need for a theological and sociological approach to the various discourses present in Latin American Christianity which might both be faithful to the Church's teaching and Scripture, and adequate to people's experience of immersion in, and desire to make sense of, a world which abounds in "sacred violence."

I could not but be very grateful indeed to Guido Delran, O.P., the director of the Instituto Pedro de Córdoba, who invited me to give the course which has turned into this book. His support and friendship in moments of darkness and tribulation are impressed into these pages in ways which few but he will understand. At the same time I would like to thank Edward Ruane, O.P., and the Dominican Community of St. Pius in Chicago for the delight and respite of the sabbatical period they granted me, which enabled me to translate and prepare the English-language edition of the text. I would also like to acknowledge the proximity between some sections of this book, particularly from chapters 2, 3, and 6, and passages from my own *The Joy of Being Wrong* (as yet unpublished). It was while working on this latter text, about Original Sin, that I had some ideas concerning matters eschatological which I sought to follow through at the first available opportunity.

One of the challenges faced by the British translator of a work into an English acceptable for a North American readership is the question of inclusive language. After much thought and consultation with qualified friends, I have opted for the traditional English use of masculine pronouns to refer to God wherever the circumlocutions required by a gender-neutral language would lead to too inelegant a contortion. I am aware that this is not an adequate solution. My instinct is that all language about God is inadequate, but it may be less obviously so if the image is unashamedly anthropomorphic. For instance, I know of no one who is led astray by the notion that God is an old man with a white beard — it's so obviously not the case that it does no harm to use the image, while to talk of God as "the ground of our being" or some such terminology might be more misleading since it gives the impression of being closer to the mark, when it is in fact no less anthropomorphic than the more patently childish image. I apologize in advance to those who do not share my criteria and for whom the juxtaposition of divinity and masculine pronouns is a source of pain and stumbling, asking them for a generous reading. The criteria adopted are an attempt at a temporary resolution of a felt difficulty rather than a definitive statement or *prise de position.*

I have generally used the Authorized, or King James, Version of the Bible for quotations from Scripture, except where I quote deuterocanonical books not found in that compilation. This, given the plethora of modern English translations available to us, may strike the reader as odd. My reasons are that the seventeenth-century text, with its sonority and splendor, is foundational to such bits of religious language as survive in the scattered memories of religion and of God of many of those whose first language is English. This is particularly true of the more apocalyptic texts, and it is these memories, and the attitudes which they inspire, with which I seek to work. It is the King James texts that are very often preferred by certain religious groups who expound them in ways more or less directly opposed to the revelation of the true God, and since what I attempt to offer is an alternative to this cultural phenomenon, it seems appropriate to do so within the terms of reference of its expositors. There are places where the Authorized Version is inadequate to the original tongues, or where its language has become so archaic as to be not only curious but downright misleading. In such places I have edited it myself, making some effort not to clash with the Jacobean tone of what I have left in place.

I am especially grateful to Mary Nugent, O.P., for her stylistic advice and her help with the correction of the text, to Diana Culbertson, O.P., for some important suggestions, and to Daniel O'Grady, Richard de Ranitz, O.P., John Gerlach, O.P., Matthew Walsh, O.P., Jerry Cleator, O.P., and Daniel Davis, O.P., for their support, generosity, and encouragement during the period of elaboration. My warmest thanks also to Mike Leach and John Eagleson of Crossroad, whose friendly enthusiasm and sheer professionalism have done so much to improve this text and make it available.

This book is dedicated to the memory of my friend Laércio Donato dos Reis (1961–94). The original version was finished in what turned out to be the last few weeks of his life, but I was unable to share its contents with the one who opened up so much life for me. These pages are both the flowers that I have not been able to lay on his grave in Brazil and my attempt to say that the stone has been rolled away. What follows is a distant stammering of the reality I hope to share with him in joy forever.

Fix Your Minds...

In the epistle to the Colossians we read this verse:

> Fix your minds [*phroneite*] on the things that are above, and not on the things of earth. (Col. 3:2)

If you know what this means, then you need spend no longer reading through these pages, for you have already received and understood the eschatological imagination. Theology is perhaps for those of us who can't find an obvious sense in what may be very simple perceptions, ones which are understood intuitively by better Christians than ourselves; theology would be for those of us who are obliged to the hard labor of dragging our obstinate intellects through the spines and thistles of our own self-deceit so as to bring each thought, each remnant of intellectual pride, captive before Christ (2 Cor. 10:5), ploughing out meaning from arid and sterile soil.

In fact the verse which I quoted belongs to a context, within which we are told:

> If then you have risen with Christ, seek the things which are above, where Christ is seated at the right hand of God.
> (Col. 3:1)

Then follows our verse, and then we get:

> For you have died and your life is hidden with Christ in God. When Christ, who is our life appears, then shall you also appear with him in glory. (Col. 3:3–4)

There is a whole nexus of references here, hidden just beneath the surface of these verses. We are told that Christ is seated at the right hand of God. This is not information about heavenly table protocol, but a reference to Psalm 110, a psalm that was of great significance for the early Christians. In Psalm 110 "the Lord says to my Lord:

'sit at my right.' " This was of particular importance to the apostolic group because Jesus himself had commented on it, immediately before his passion, in the Temple. He had insinuated that the Messiah, the son of David, was, in fact, the Lord, seated at the right hand of God (Mark 12:35–37 and parallels). The apostolic group, remembering this, understood after the resurrection that Jesus had prophesied what would become of him by means of this psalm. We know that, because they described the way in which the risen Lord ceased to appear to them and rose into heaven, in terms of this psalm.

This can be seen in passages like Romans 8:34; Ephesians 1:20; Hebrews 1:3, 13; and 1 Peter 3:22. We are talking about something which was evidently imbued with great significance for the apostolic witnesses to the life and resurrection of Jesus: the happening which we describe when, while professing our faith, we say, "He ascended into heaven and is seated at the right hand of God." That is to say, we are talking about the Ascension. Well indeed, and what might *that* mean? Is that happening in any way significant to us? We are used to a certain discourse about the cross, perhaps a somewhat sick one, and also a discourse about the resurrection, perhaps a somewhat vacuous one. But, a discourse about the Ascension? Insofar as it gets talked about at all it appears as a somewhat apologetic loose end to the resurrection stories, as if it were a slightly shameful way of explaining why Jesus is no longer to be found, at least in this form. Certainly I'm not aware of much importance being attached to this happening, and even less of anyone attributing to it a marked incidence in our lives.

However, it seems to have a special importance in the apostolic witness; in fact, in the verse which I quoted at the beginning it seems to be the *sine qua non* by which Christians understand who we are, as well as being a principle of action. If this is the case, then we are talking about some lost understanding, something that was quite clear for the apostolic witnesses, but which has become so opaque for us that we don't even realize that we're missing out on something. So, we're going to do a little bit of detective work, rather like an archaeological dig, with the difference that instead of looking for a criminal or for the remains of an ancient building, we are seeking to bring out traces of the lost inner dynamic of a series of texts which we have available to us.

Now, this is no easy exercise, since our temptation with any ancient text is to find ourselves reflected in it. This can't be avoided, since we cannot draw close to any text except as ourselves, with all our education, our insights, our psychology, prejudices, and resentments. However, in the case of this text, the text of the apostolic witness, which we normally call "The New Testament," the Church, as the original compiler of the text, asks us to go slow. We are told that something extraordinary and indescribable took place with the person of Jesus of Nazareth, and that this happening produced a series of changes in the way of perceiving things and carrying them out in the people who had known and accompanied him. These people, or rather their friends and collaborators, put into writing something of what they had experienced, and these writings are conserved with immense care by the Church. From time to time the Church becomes aware that it doesn't understand very well certain parts of its own vital text; however, it clings on to it, since it realizes that, whatever that original experience was, it still happens today, and it still transforms the perceptions of those who are affected by it. That means that when we look at this text we are asked to tread with care, like Moses before the bush, so that we don't fail to notice that this text, unlike most other texts, is capable of subverting our education, of altering our perception, and of questioning our prejudices and resentments. When we say that this text is "Holy Scripture," we don't mean to say that it is venerable, with a patina of glorious tradition, or something like that. We mean that we don't question it so as to break it, but rather we allow it to get close enough to us to produce a break in us. If we can hear the parts of the text which make no sense, rather than only those parts which we use to justify ourselves and strengthen our self-image, then perhaps from within that same sense of strangeness we will hear the Other whose image we are called to recover.

What we're going to do, then, is to allow some texts of the apostolic witness to question us, so as to see what kind of imagination was at work in some of those which offer us no obvious sense. It may be that the discovery of a meaning will show us a series of insights about ourselves and our lives, and, difficult though it may seem, the possibility of new attitudes, new directions. To carry this out any reader must be honest about the method he or she is using, that is to say, what some of the presuppositions are that are being brought to the text. So I'm going to try to set out before you the tools which I'll be using to try to recover the inner dynamic of the apostolic witness, tools which are to be found in the mimetic theory of René Girard.

A Bird's-Eye View of Mimetic Theory

Mimetic theory is a particular understanding of human relationships which implies, at the same time, a way of understanding human culture. That is to say that it offers a simultaneous perception of what moves human beings in their relationships and of what forms them in the structures that are previous to, and often hidden from, their relationships. Perhaps it will help us to get a perspective on this if we say that this single idea helps to break the barrier between two approaches to our self-understanding which haven't, up until now, been able to find an inner link: the psychological approach, following Freud, which concentrates on the individual person, conceiving his or her problems as internal to that person, and the sociological approach, which conceives of problems as "out there" — objective, independent of your or my motives, of our intentions, feelings, and so on. You realize, I imagine, and even if you haven't given it much thought, that this split has marked effects on theology: consider the way in which the discourse about sin used to be confined to the world of the "personal," and then how there was an attempt to rescue it from that sphere so as to emphasize it as something "structural," an attempt which, for reasons that may become clearer as we progress, has not yielded the fruit that was hoped for.

Anyhow, mimetic theory proposes a way of understanding humans which is simultaneously personal and social, since it treats the person as absolutely dependent on the other, both social and personal, who is previous to it. Thus it conceives of the relationality between this "other" and the person as absolutely key to any understanding of what's going on. I'm going to try to describe this way of focusing on the human being in the simplest possible terms. The first question which it puts to us is: how do you desire? The reply is: I desire in imitation of somebody. For something to have value or interest for me, someone, another, has to have given it that value or interest. This process begins in all our cases in the tenderest infancy, when it was in fact the process of imitation in all of us, moved by a gravitational attraction to another, which led us to articulate sounds and make gestures. It was the capacity to repeat sounds which led to the formation of memory, and thence to language, since there is no language without memory. That is to say that the very possibility of our being conscious creatures at all is owed to the mechanism of imitation. We imitate not only what people do and how they appear, but we are also moved by an even stronger gravitational pull: a desire to be. In the event of good parenting, the baby is permitted to receive a sense of being and doesn't have to grasp to receive this sense of being. At the other end of the spectrum there are infants who receive no sense of being, and for whom years can pass during which they search in every possible way, locked into many painful and exacerbated repetitive mechanisms, to acquire a sense of being. Most of us are somewhere on the scale between those whose sense of being, whose "I," was pacifically loved into being, so that they can imitate those who love them into existence in a pacific way, with few conflicts, and those who feel they have to grasp at a sense of being which always eludes them, manipulating and controlling others in their search. Certainly no one is entirely without some sense of struggle, some violent acquisition of self.

This means to say that our desires are acquired in imitation of the desires of others, that the "I" who is called into being depends entirely on the others who surround him or her. The "I" which nurtures the mirage of its own originality, blind to its dependence, is perhaps the one who is most dependent on the desires of others, but in hidden and compulsive ways. Well, so far no problem. But that means that we are always predisposed to conflict. Consider this: if I recognize my absolute dependence on the other for my desire, in both the personal and the social sphere, then I am at peace with the other. However, the moment I seek to affirm that my desire is previous and original, then I'm in a conflictual relationship with the other. A trivial example: a member of my group appears with some new jeans of a certain brand. It's someone I like and admire: I'd like to be like him; if I were like him, then perhaps I'd be more desirable, more attractive, myself. Perhaps I might even "be" a bit more. So, I buy the same jeans, and, of course the others in the group comment: "Look, you've imitated Tom, you've bought the same jeans." Now, if I were that extraordinarily rare and sane thing, a humble and simple person, I'd reply: "Yes, you're right. I like Tom, and I'd like to be more like him." However, it's more probable that 99 percent of us would reply: "You're crazy; no way am I imitating him. I saw these jeans in the shop, or on TV, before he even suspected their existence. I just didn't have the money at the time." So I affirm that my desire was previous and original, and I deny my real dependence on the other. This is something absolutely simple, and is well understood by the world of advertising, which rarely seeks to leave you with a simple description of a product. Rather it seeks to seduce you into desiring it by showing you someone attractive, who clearly has being, spark, or whatever, enjoying life with their product. Message: If you buy X, then you can be like Y, that is to say, really *live*.

Well, that's fine while there are plenty of Xs for sale. But what if it's not Tom's jeans which I like, but his girlfriend? Isn't this just a typical scene from adolescence! Tom and Frank are close friends and have been since childhood. As he gets to adolescence, Tom, who has a brother a couple of years older than he who already has a girl-friend, begins to try going out with a girl. He's in love, or at least convinced that he ought to be in love, so he goes on and on about the girl in the most exaggerated tones. The object of the exercise is to convince Frank that she's the most wonderful girl in the world, since Tom can't imagine desiring something that Frank doesn't desire as well; after all, thus far they've desired everything together: their music, their sports, their first cigarettes, and so on. At first Frank is not going to be impressed. Here is Tom desiring an object in which he, Frank can't participate, since, after all a girlfriend isn't like a fashion or a cigarette. She's indivisible. However, Frank is used to learning to desire following his friendship with Tom, and suddenly, led on by his friendship with Tom, he begins to perceive that, in fact, she does have a certain appeal, and suddenly, what a surprise, Frank falls for her! Of course, at this stage, he fights with Tom, who can't under-stand how his best friend could do such a thing to him. Tom takes his distance, losing his interest in the girl. At that moment Frank also discovers that he's lost interest in her: his interest depended on Tom. When Tom is distant, as friend and as rival, the girl loses her inter-est. Well, this story, where the male and female rôles can be changed around at pleasure, is so transparent that we all understand it at once: we all desire through the eyes of another.

This has brought us to the threshold of conflict. Let's try another story to understand better what's going on. Now we have a brilliant professor and a brilliant pupil. The pupil imitates the teacher, and this flatters the professor, and she likes it, and so she encourages the pupil. So far no rivalry, no conflict. However, as the pupil be-comes ever more successful, the professor gets alarmed. She begins to fear for her own position and enters into rivalry with her own pupil, complicating things for her, making a ferocious critique of a brilliant seminar which the pupil gave. The pupil is disoriented: why is this happening to me? Why is my faithful imitation and love for my teacher rewarded in this way? She continues to try to imitate, but now finds that she's a rival to her own model, who has entered into rivalry with her. They fall out, apparently over some vital point of truth to do with the interpretation of black holes, or the text of Aristotle. In fact the quarrel has no real reason why. It is irrational; it has to do with the rivalry between the two.

Now let's imagine that their quarrel is causing chaos in the faculty, and that they need to patch things up in some way so that a government agency doesn't deprive them of funds. If they were people of extraordinary humility and simplicity they could, of course, each go to the other and say: "I'm sorry, I see that the problem is that I've been in rivalry with you, which is entirely unnecessary, and I must learn to love without envy, imitating pacifically." However, if they were so simple and humble, it's unlikely that the squabble would have arisen in the first place. Rather, they adopt a different approach to resolving their conflict. "Look, our conflict would never have arisen if it depended on us alone; in fact it was that visiting professor from Venezuela who has sowed conflict between us. If we manage to get rid of him, then our faculty will know peace." So, they do exactly that, fully convinced that the Venezuelan in question was the source of all the troubles in the faculty. They must really believe that he truly was the source, for if they don't, they won't manage to make peace. In fact, yes, they do reach agreement, with a completely objective analysis, about blaming the Venezuelan. They throw him out and suddenly find that in their faculty peace reigns. What they haven't perceived is that it's a fake peace, based on a deceit, and that eventually their rivalry, which has only been covered over with a Band-Aid, will break out again, and they'll have to repeat the mechanism again, sacrificing, this time, Lord alone knows which expendable victim.

Well, there we have mimetic theory. It says that all human culture and society are like that, that all humans desire in this way, and that the way by which we produce peace is by the expulsion of someone held to be responsible for our conflicts. That is to say we are all, always and everywhere, immensely violent creatures, and the only way which we have to control this violence is the search for collective unanimity against a victim. We can imagine a founding murder of this type, of the sort that can be detected in much human mythology, and so observe the process in its entirety. A group enters into conflict and there is a threat of chaos. Mysteriously there occurs a spontaneous movement which unites everybody against someone who is easy to victimize (that is, who can't take vengeance). That person is killed, and immediately peace is restored. The group cannot perceive that it is its own unanimous violence which has produced the peace, because that would be to recognize the innocence of the victim, and the chance, random nature of its selection. So the magic peace is attributed to the victim, who was perceived as violent and the cause of all problems while with the group and who, once gone, bequeaths peace to the group. Conclusion: we were visited by a god, an ambiguous god, previously terrible, now beneficent. We must establish three things to maintain peace: first, we must prohibit all the sorts of behavior which led to the group conflict (which means principally special prohibitions against the sorts of imitative behavior which lead to conflict). Secondly, we must repeat, insofar as possible, the original expulsion which led to our peace. So we produce a rite which consists of a well-controlled mime of an act of mass-violence which ends in the immolation of some victim, originally human, later animal, and so on. In the third place we must tell the story of how we were visited by the gods and founded as a group and as a people, and so we give birth to myth.

This means that social prohibition is essentially a violent form of protection against violence, made possible by a murder, that ritual is essentially a disguised mime of a murder, and that myth is the story of a lynch-death told from the perspective of the persecutors. Now this whole system of producing and maintaining meaning, which can be found in the rites and myths spread all over our planet, depends on only one absolutely indispensable element. That is: a blindness on the part of the participants with respect to what they're really doing when they kill the victim. In other words, an authentic belief in the guilt of the victim. The whole cultural system, and everything in it, depends on this blindness, without which there would be no way to resolve conflicts, and societies would self-destruct.

There is, of course, only one way by which it can come to be perceived that an entire culture is founded on a lie that is related to a murder. That is when someone with an entirely different perception, someone whose perception is not formed by that lie, comes to the group, and points this out to them. In the case of our human history there has only been one perception which has genuinely flowed against the current of all the other stories and myths, and that is the Jewish story, which consists in the long, slow discovery of the innocence of the victim. We can see this very clearly if we compare the story of Romulus and Remus, the story of the foundation of Rome, with the story of Cain and Abel, the story of the foundation of human culture. In the first story two indistinguishable brothers fight about who's going to found Rome. They organize a competition to determine which is the first to see a sign from heaven. Remus saw some birds, and then Romulus saw some other, more impressive, birds. In the fight which ensued Romulus killed Remus and became the founder of Rome. Remus was blamed for his impiety toward the gods and for that reason Romulus was right to kill him. In the book of Genesis there are two indistinguishable brothers. One kills the other, and so founds human culture. Thus far the two stories are identical: the Bible and the myth agree that human culture is rooted in murder. However, with an identical structure there is a difference of interpretation, and it is all the difference in the world. God says to Cain: "Where is your brother? His blood cries out to me from the soil." That means that the murder is no more than that: a sordid crime, impossible to justify; and God is on the side of the victim and doesn't help to mystify Cain's self-deception.

We could, of course, work through the Bible and see how it is, all too frequently, just the same as all the myths of our planet, with God scarcely different from the gods. However, little by little the process of the dis-covery, the un-covering, of the victim is worked, and so is the subversion of the story told by the persecutors, so that the innocence of the victim is made ever clearer. Consider the story of Joseph, the book of Job, the extraordinary "Songs of the Suffering Servant" in Isaiah. Little by little God is distinguished from the violence of the gods, and is perceived to be on the side of the victim. This is the genius of Judaism, and it has no strict equivalent in any other people or culture. We're talking about what we often call "revelation": God's self-revelation in the opening of our eyes so that we see what we do when we sacralize victims; God revealing himself by means of the innocent victim. In the Old Testament we never reach a full revelation of the innocence of the victim, nor a full separation of God from involvement in the "sacred," which is to say in self-deceiving violence. That fullness of revelation occurs only in the life, death, and resurrection of Jesus.

The New Testament is exactly the same story as all the myths of our planet: a time of crisis, an attempt to save the situation by producing the unanimous expulsion of a victim, and then the semi-legalized lynching of that victim. The structure is identical to that of the very many myths and stories of foundation which we could examine. There is one single difference: exactly the same story is being told from the inverse perspective. It is the story from the perspective of the victim. The victim is proclaimed innocent. We are told that it was envy that led to his death. He fulfilled a prophecy that he would be hated without cause, that he would be counted among sinners, unjustly. His lynch-death would not produce a new peace and social order as his executioners had hoped, with their magnificent motto:

It is expedient for us that one man should die for the people and that the whole nation perish not. (John 11:50)

The murderous lie is exposed in its entirety.

Not only that, but it is apparent that the victim was not "canonized," so to speak, after his death: "He had been a bad influence, but came to be perceived as a good influence afterward." Rather it came to be perceived that he had been good from the beginning and that he had known and understood exactly the mechanism which would lead to his death. He had prepared his followers for this and taught them how to avoid participating in just such movements toward a lynch. He taught them, in fact, how to leave behind being run by the sort of conflictual imitative desire which we saw earlier and, at the same time, how to take the place of the excluded, those who are being made, or could easily be made, into victims. The whole of mimetic theory is turned upside down by just one person.

I hope that this brief gallop through mimetic theory is comprehensible. It has, as you have seen, three "moments" in a single package. First, there is the "moment" of imitative triangular desire: when I desire an object in imitation of the desire of another, and so enter into conflict. Then comes the "moment" of the scapegoat mechanism, by which conflict is resolved in a human group by the unanimous expulsion of a victim. The final "moment" is the subversion from within of this universal mechanism by the slow irruption within human history of an "Other" of a different sort than the violent "other" which normally forms our desire, culminating in the visible acting out, the *mise-en-scène* of what that "Other" really is by a man who goes to his death so as to un-cover the founding lie.

Well, thus far mimetic theory, which you will notice as a sort of constant backdrop to this book, and to which I'll make allusion or reference with some frequency. It is an insight into the workings of human relationships at both a cultural and a personal level which occurred to René Girard, and since he elaborated it, it has been studied and applied in a whole host of different disciplines: economy, psychology, ethnology, theology, political science, literary criticism, and so on. We're going to put it to work to see what it helps us to recover from the apostolic witness: that is to say, we're putting it to theological use. To do this we have to return to first principles and ask ourselves what it is which makes this story, this theory, possible in the first place.

How Do We Know the Innocence of the Victim?

What happened to enable us to understand the innocence of the victim? That's the same question as this one: what was it that made it possible that the apostolic group could write their accounts of the life and death of the man Jesus of Nazareth? And what was it that brought about the immense change in consciousness, in perception, and in imagination with relation to God, to what it is to be human, to history which makes of their texts something without strict comparison in the literature and the myths of our planet? Let us not forget that there are some things which seem natural enough to us but which are, in fact, culturally unique and simply do not exist outside the cultural world which has been touched by the Christian texts. For example, when we read an account of a great disaster, we don't ask, "Who is responsible?" but "What happened?," expecting a scientific answer rather than that some victim be sacrificed to placate the disaster. This attitude, the search for causes other than those that can be remedied by a little expulsion, a little lynching, seems obvious to us. However, we're unique in this, even in our wars, military and economic, when we think that victims have rights. We are not very effective when it comes to making their rights worth something, but even the less sensitive among us would be shocked by life in a society like that of ancient Rome where the defeated would be killed or enslaved without further ado. They had no rights: that's what "being defeated" meant.

Well, what was it that produced this development? The answer is, of course, the same thing which made Jesus *not* be to his disciples just one more dead man, crushed by human violence and probably cursed by God as well, a very dangerous sinner. The answer is the resurrection. Here we are talking about a historical happening, the appearance to the apostolic group over a certain period of time beginning the Sunday after his death of the same man whom they had known up until his death. It was this historical happening which irrupted into the midst of the apostolic group which put into movement that immense change of perception that we're going to explore. That is to say, we're talking in the first place not about an idea, not even about a memory or a feeling, but about a historical experience, something which happened to a certain group of people and of which they began to tell others. And, in the process of beginning to tell, they began to discover that what had happened was not only interesting in itself, but also changed a whole series of perceptions of more or less the whole of human reality. These apostolic witnesses finally put their testimony into writing, and it is this which we conserve and call the New Testament. These texts bear witness both to what they're talking about and to what gives them their structure. Both things are interesting. What they talk about is the life, death, and resurrection of Jesus of Nazareth. What gives them their structure is the growing perception that the resurrection of the victim made possible a certain intelligence, a certain perspective on things, which Jesus had had before his death and which began to possess the apostolic group after the resurrection.

If you look at chapter 1 of my book *Knowing Jesus,*[1] you'll find a look at the effects of the appearances of the risen Lord to the apostolic group. Here I'd just like to fill that in a little. Let us remember that Jesus had given a series of teachings and interpretations concerning God which, although formally impeccable on every point, when they were taken together had certainly seemed dangerous to the guardians of the Law. It was clear that Jesus' teaching and way of behaving threatened the difference between those "inside" and those "outside," between the good and the bad, thus seeming to dissolve order, with all the things which upheld it like the Temple, the Sabbath, ritual prescriptions, and so on. Finally, in his teaching Jesus imparted a new perception of God, whom he called his Father. He also claimed to be an authentic witness to God, whom he said was revealed in his own words and in his works. Given this, it was most probable that he was blasphemous and was certainly leading people astray, giving them motive to depart from the path given to God's people by Moses and the Prophets. If he worked miracles, then these were probably from the devil, as part of a snare and a deception for God's people.

Now it's possible that Jesus' disciples may have been pretty cynical with relation to the authorities, religious and others, in Israel. However, it's extremely unlikely that, when he died, they didn't come to accept something of those authorities' point of view about Jesus.

---

1. James Alison, *Knowing Jesus* (London: SPCK, 1993; Springfield, Ill.: Templegate, 1994).

Death is final and puts to an end the voice of the dissident, making those who killed him or her seem decent and reasonable people: after all one's got to carry on living with them. The disciples on their way to Emmaus were sunk in the grief of those for whom Jesus' death was the triumph of the point of view of his persecutors. This viewpoint worked like this: this Jesus was a sinner, and in killing him, God's will was being done, since he had broken God's law. His death included hanging on a tree which meant, according to Deuteronomy (Deut. 21:23; cf. Gal. 3:13), that he died under the curse of God.

Naturally, then, if such a person rises from the dead and appears to his disciples, the whole system of thought which had led to his execution is called into question. In the first place it means that Jesus had been right in the testimony which he had given about God: God is indeed the one who Jesus had described and that means that God is not like Jesus' adversaries had claimed him to be. So the reasons given for doing away with Jesus were not reasons, but part of a sinful human mechanism for getting rid of people, which has nothing to do with God. When this mechanism adduces that a death like this is a sign of God's curse, then its claim is quite simply mistaken; this raises the question of whether the Law really does reflect God truly, or whether it has not rather been distorted by human violence.

I'm going to try to say this even more clearly: Jesus' resurrection did not only reveal that this man was, in fact, innocent; it did not only reveal that Jesus was right about God. It did much more: it revealed the whole mechanism by which innocent victims are created by people who think that by creating such victims they are working God's most holy will. That is to say, it left wide open the murderous and mendacious nature of all human religion, even in its best and purest form, the one practiced by those who are, in truth, the chosen people of God, the bearers of God's revelation.[2] It was this perception which permitted the apostolic witnesses to apply to Jesus the verse which is found in Psalms 35 and 69:

They hated me without a cause (John 15:25)

and also the quotation from Isaiah 53:

He was reckoned among the transgressors. (Luke 22:37).

---

2. I note that the self-criticism which this realization inspires, and which historical Christianity has notoriously practiced far too infrequently, could only have seen the light of day in the midst of the chosen people, whose special genius it is.

The application of these verses to a man killed as a criminal can be understood only if the whole nature of the mechanism which led to his death has been unveiled, exposed for what it really is. It has become possible to imagine the complete innocence of the victim, which means, of course, the complete complicity in violence of the lynchers.

Now I ask you each to imagine yourselves as members of the apostolic group, feeling that in some way Jesus hadn't been up to fulfilling your hopes and that, when all is said and done, the authorities, hateful though they be, may have been right, and Jesus did not come from God. Then the risen Jesus appears to you and your friends. How do you talk about this? The question isn't as silly as it seems. We can all tell stories, and our stories have beginnings and ends, and Jesus' story had its end, a sad end, but at least an end. This is part of our human experience: our stories are ritualized in the same way as our lives, by the way in which our culture is bound in by death. How do we tell a story about someone who died and then rose again? It's not at all clear, since we have no model for such a story, no ready-made recipe to follow. We have to change our whole conception of the stories we tell, which is pretty fundamental since not only are we animals who tell stories, but it is the stories we tell about ourselves and about others which make possible that we act in the way in which, in fact, we act. How are we going to tell a story which has no end, at least as far as we know such ends? To ask this question is, already, to ask about the eschatological imagination, which is what we're trying to do in this book. We are trying to observe the apostolic group's developing attempt to tell Jesus' story when there is no known way to tell a story that is not girded about by death, and we are trying to do this because we cannot do without it if we are to try to tell the same story as they, which is to say, if we are to be faithful to the teaching of the apostles.

What I'm claiming is that there is only one reason that a Christian eschatology exists at all, and that is the resurrection. The resurrection was the irruption into the midst of the normal human story, shot through with death, of a rather different story, one which we do not know how to tell very well. This means that the study of eschatology is an attempt to study the fullness of the density of the resurrection. The question about the Ascension which I raised at the beginning of this chapter is a question about one of the dimensions of the resurrection. Our intention is not to study anything else in these pages. We're going to do this not only by looking at the texts of the resurrection in the Gospels, but by looking at the change and development in the way the apostolic group told the story of Jesus as the density of the resurrection made it impossible for them to tell the old story and obliged them to invent new ways of speaking, new structures of telling and of writing stories, the ones which we have in the New Testament.

The second point which I would like to emphasize with relation to the appearances of the risen Lord is that he didn't appear to his disciples just as someone who had been dead, but was now better and risen. That would be a pretty story, but a somewhat cheap one, and it would fit in with stories which we know how to tell about people who were ill, and then get better, or people who disappear and then reappear. In contrast to this, the risen Jesus was dead. I'm not talking about some horror-film mummy wandering about: it clearly wasn't like that. When Luke and John tell us that the risen Lord appeared with the visible wounds of his death, it wasn't merely a way of identifying him as the same person but a way of affirming that he was so much the same person, that, in the same way as that person was dead, so was he. But that death is nothing but a vacant form for God, something whose reality has been utterly emptied out, which can only be detected in the form of its traces in the human life story of someone who has overcome death.

The marks, then, of Jesus' death were something like trophies: it was his whole human life, including his death, which was made alive and presented before the disciples as a sign that he had in fact conquered death. This not only meant that he had personally conquered death, which he had manifestly done, but that, in addition, the whole mechanism by which death retains people in its thrall had been shown to be unnecessary. Whatever death is, it is not something which has to structure every human life from within (as in fact it does), but rather it is an empty shell, a bark without a bite. None of us has any reason to fear being dead, something which will unquestionably happen to all of us, since that state cannot separate us effectively from the real source of life. This can scarcely be said with more precision than it is by the author of the epistle to the Hebrews:

Forasmuch then as the children are partakers of flesh and blood, he also himself likewise took part of the same; that through death he might destroy him that had the power of death, that is, the devil; and deliver them who through fear of death were all their lifetime subject to bondage. (Heb. 2:14–15)

Now I insist on this, since it is the central pillar of the Catholic faith. From the presence to the disciples of the risen victim, the crucified one risen *as crucified,* the lamb triumphant *as slaughtered,* everything else flows. Without that insight, nothing unfolds, no clear perception of God, of grace, of eternal life, about what we must do, how we must live. This means that eschatology is an attempt to understand ever more fully the relationship between those empty marks of death which Jesus bore and the mysterious splendor of the human bodily life which enabled them to be seen. What type of life is it that is capable not of canceling death out, which would be to stay on the same level as it, but to include it, making a trophy of it, allowing it to be something that can be shown to others so that they be not afraid? It is about this that I wish to speak. Remember please that this presence of Christ risen as crucified is the centerpoint of our investigation. Perhaps at some stage I'll give the impression of wandering away from it; but if I really have, then I'll have lost my way. In fact we'll be chewing over it, coming back to it, moving out from it, seeking to allow it to cast light on our texts, trying to see how this presence, which seems so elusive to us, is in fact the pivot of everything, what makes it possible that there is a story to tell at all, what makes it possible that we find sense, or meaning, at all.

The Principle of Analogy

Well, that gives us some idea of what we'll be trying to unpack in the pages that follow. Now, please allow me to give a hint as to my method before we move on. It's a small note about what is usually called the principle of analogy, without which there would be no Catholic theology. We can imagine someone who has followed me thus far interrupting me and saying: "What you say is quite true, and brings us to a simple conclusion. You're right to say that the human story which we know and tell is one which is entirely hemmed in by death, and thus by futility and vanity. When God raised Jesus from the dead, all our human stories were shown to be completely vain, to have nothing to do with God. In place of these God revealed himself in the risen Jesus, and thus gives a story, to which we have access only through the words of Scripture, which we have to tell repeatedly, even when we scarcely understand the words, until he returns, and brings about the promised new heavens and the new earth."

The person who says this is denying the principle of analogy. He or she is denying that there is any correspondence at all between the earthly story, which culminates in the self-deception leading to the lynch, and the heavenly story, which according to our imaginary speaker simply covers over and annuls the earthly story for those of us lucky enough to be caught up in the breaking in of the ineffable and incomprehensible heavenly story. This way of speaking imagines the resurrection to be the overcoming of death, but not its assumption. The risen Christ is merely at another level, strange and mysterious, and death has simply been abolished by God. According to this vision, so great is human violence that it is just not possible for us to speak of, or imagine, the risen life in which there is no violence at all. However, in fact, one of the principal senses of the presence of the crucified and risen victim is to show that it is all of human history, *including its murderous vanity,* that has been taken up into the resurrection life. The temptation of speaking in a way that ignores this "taking up" is especially strong in certain of the forms of Christianity that were born at the time of the Reformation. However, it is not the only temptation.

The second temptation is perhaps much more present in a certain Catholicism, one which makes much use of Aristotle and a certain understanding of St. Thomas Aquinas, one which lays much stress on the "natural law," conceived in such a way as to make it almost indistinguishable from the Jewish Law, which Paul very well understood to have become an instrument of death. By contrast with the first temptation, this one makes use of the language of analogy, insisting that there is a real analogy between the human story and the divine, so much so that human reason can, without much difficulty, understand divine things, that it is not so hard for human laws to be a reflection of the divine will, and so on. We can imagine a representative of this school of thought saying to us: "Well, yes, but you're exaggerating the violence and the self-deception of humanity; in fact we aren't so bad, and to insist that we are is to fail to give God the glory due to him for the goodness of creation." In psychology this is called "denial": when a person, in order to cover over the pain and the memory of some terrible wound produced by the abuse or negligence of that person's parents or guardians, denies, in good faith, the existence of the pain and is only capable of speaking well of the parent in question, even though he or she speak in somewhat static and defensive terms.

In fact God does not need us to deny the violence which surrounds and permeates us in order to give him glory. But if we do follow that path, we seriously underestimate the fact that it was only by over-coming death that God could give himself to be known by us in something approximating his fullness. We underestimate the element of violence which is present in human life. When we speak about the resurrection, we emphasize the similarity, the physical appearance, of the risen Christ, but play down the way in which that physical appearance was frequently unrecognizable for the disciples, was un-questionably something other. In short, according to this temptation, the element of violence is, indeed, present in human life, but not so present as to make of the risen life something radically different from what we already know and live.

Both these temptations are strong, and both have a number of practical moral and pastoral consequences. Neither of the two really portrays the Catholic faith, as I understand it, the faith in the cru-cified and risen victim: the first because it denies the possibility of a real relationship between the human and the divine stories, and the second because it sees too easy a relationship between the two. It seems to me that the presence of the crucified and risen victim sug-gests that in fact the divine story is related to the human story, but *as its subversion from within.* That is to say that human violence, the dominion of death, is so powerful that we can't tell the divine story at all. However God, by becoming human, created a real human story which is the celestial subversion from within of our violent history, and as such we can find points of contact with it, because it is the turning inside-out of our story, the construction of a story that is not that of a violent lynching, but of a peaceful un-lynching, so to speak. For the divine story to be at all comprehensible to us we need it to start from, and make use of, the story that we do know how to tell, but only insofar as it enables us to begin to tell a story that must always include the human overcoming of that story.

That seems to me to be part of what Jesus' appearance with the marks of death visible in his risen flesh means. The heavenly story is not just at a different level — the abolition of the human story — but starting from that moment it includes that which is capable of being rescued and transformed: the human story of violence and victimiza-tion. We could say that God has committed himself to heaven being a human story which will forever include the story of the human overcoming of death by Jesus. This seems to me to be tremendously important for our personal lives. An English mystic of the Middle Ages, Julian of Norwich, the appreciation for whose thought is on the increase as her insights are recovered, affirms that in heaven our sins will be not shame, but glory to us. This seems to me to be the authentically Catholic intuition. I try to make sense of it in terms of the transvestite prostitutes whom I knew in Brazil when they were in the final phase of their struggle with AIDS. I hope to know them again in heaven, not so transmogrified that their personal life story has been, in each case, abolished, but rather so utterly alive that their fake beauty, arduously cultivated, their sad personal stories of envy, violence, frustration in love, and their illness have become trophies which are not sources of shame, but which add to their beauty and their joy.

Let this do for a start. This whole book is structured around this principle of analogy: God's revelation is known thanks to a subversion from within of human violence. This will be the central axis, so to speak, around which our reflections will gyrate. In the next chapter we will begin to look at the way in which the presence of the risen victim subverted the apostolic group's perception of God from within.

The Living God

In the first chapter we saw that the purpose of this book is to enable us to have some insight into what might be meant by fixing the mind on the things that are above. From there we moved on to look at the understanding of human relationships which its discoverer, René Girard, has called mimetic theory. This seeks to understand the imitative and triangular nature of desire, the mechanism of the randomly chosen scapegoat, and the overcoming of this mechanism by God's self-revelation as a human victim. We ended with a look at the central factor which enables there to be a Christian story, and thus a Christian theology, at all: the presence to the apostolic group of Jesus, the crucified and risen victim.

Now we are going to try to examine the way in which the presence of the risen Jesus among the apostolic witnesses began to make possible a change in the human perception of God: what we might call an authentic human discovery about God. Consider the following example concerning the Anglo-Indian writer Salman Rushdie. This author, who is technically a Muslim because his father was one, was judged by some of the competent authorities to be blasphemous against Islamic belief on account of some remarks of his in a book entitled *The Satanic Verses*. The Ayatollah Khomeini then applied to him formally the death sentence which Islamic Law prescribes for the Muslim who blasphemes: any Muslim who comes across him has not only the right, but the duty, to kill him, and this in the name of Allah, the just, the merciful.

Behind the *Fatwa,* or decree, of the Ayatollah, which began with the invocation of Allah in the form I have just quoted, there is a certain understanding of God which is absolutely bound in with a mechanism of violence. That is to say: God keeps the group pure and clean by expelling from its midst any contaminating element. When the Ayatollah pronounced his sentence against Rushdie in the name of Allah, the just, the merciful, it was not, as we may be inclined to think, ever so slightly infected as we are by the texts of the New Tes-

34

tament, something ironic. For the Ayatollah, Allah precisely shows his mercy and his justice to the group by expelling the evil one. His mercy is shown to the community of the faithful by cleansing it of whatsoever impurity. Lest some anti-Islamic comment be understood here, let it be said that this understanding of mercy is that of the majority of cultures, it is the understanding which is to be found in many of the psalms, and we received a good example of it recently at the hands of the cardinal archbishop of Buenos Aires. In August 1994 this prelate proposed the creation of special ghettos for the homosexual population of Argentina, so as, in words which would have sat well on the lips of the late Ayatollah, to "clean an ignoble stain from the face of society." If we find ourselves surprised by such positions, it is not because they are rare positions, but rather because a Gospel perspective is itself, when we don't betray it, rather rare.

Here is the question which the example raises: is the god at the root of such examples the God of Jesus? Jesus himself assures us that this is not the case. The image of God which he proposes to us in the parable of the lost sheep (Luke 15:3–7) is exactly the inverse of the god we've seen. According to this parable the mercy of God is shown *not* to the group, but to the lost member, to the outsider. I ask you to consider quite how extraordinary this change of perception with respect to who God is turns out to be: mercy has been changed from something which covers up violence to something which unmasks it completely. For God there are no "outsiders," which means that any mechanism for the creation of "outsiders" is automatically and simply a mechanism of human violence, and that's that.

Jesus' Perception of God

By touching on this topic we have drawn close to the change of perception which the apostolic group underwent as a result of Jesus' resurrection. Let us begin to understand this by means of a passage which bears witness to the perception of God which Jesus himself had before his death, that shown in his debate with the Sadducees "who deny the resurrection" (Mark 12:18–27; Matt. 22:23–33; Luke 20:27–38). That this is one of the more important texts of the New Testament can be deduced from the way in which it is present in almost identical form in three of the Gospels in exactly the same place: just before the Passion. The reason that it is important is that it gives us direct information about how Jesus perceived God. This can be worked out in two ways: from what Jesus considered to be wrong, and from what he considered to be right. We will look first at what he considered to be wrong. Let us refresh our memories as to who the Sadducees were: they were "establishment" figures, for whom the only Sacred Scripture was the Pentateuch. Their position was that if there really were a resurrection, then God would have told Moses, his prophet and friend, about it, and Moses would have put it into the Pentateuch. But Moses *didn't* put it into the Pentateuch, so one can bet pretty safely that God told him nothing about this matter, and since he was God's friend, from whom something of such importance would not be hidden, this means that there is no resurrection.

However, they had better evidence still. There was a law in Deuteronomy which set out that, if a married man died without children, then it fell to his brother to take that man's widow as his wife to beget a child for his late brother and thus assure him posterity. At first sight this seems to be a piece of matrimonial law. However the Sadducees understood their own Scriptures rather better than that: this law existed exactly because the only way of bluffing past the universal reign of death was by having children. The best existence which there might be after death would be that of the shades in Sheol, which wasn't worth having. The only way to have a blessing in the land of the living was by having children, descendants. It was because of this that the man who died without children needed his brother to get for him the share in posterity that he couldn't get for himself. The Sadducees were right, in a certain sense: the existence of the levirate law is good evidence that nobody at the time it was written imagined the existence of the resurrection, since, if they had, the levirate law would have been otiose. If it was not considered otiose it was because there was no such resurrection. It's not a bad argument. Furthermore, they added an ingenious little touch to it, by producing the spectacle of seven brothers who died before having children, passing the wife on like a used car. Jewish listeners at the time would probably have thought immediately of the seven Maccabee brothers who had been executed for their refusal to abandon the Law and who were considered immortal. In fact the passage from the book of Maccabees which describes their death is one of the earliest passages in Scripture to attest to the existence of the resurrection of the dead, precisely as a prize for God's martyrs. So it's as if the Sadducees were saying: "The levirate law undercuts all arguments for the resurrection of the dead, even if you use as an example the Maccabee brothers," who were a favorite example for the partisans of the popular Jewish belief in the resurrection.

Jesus is not impressed by this really rather splendid rabbinical argument. It is worth noticing what he does *not* do. He does not answer them while accepting their insinuation about the Maccabees; he doesn't even suggest to them that their clinging to "Soli Pentateuchi" — "by the Pentateuch alone" — is a little narrow and that perhaps they might do well to take into account other, more promising, texts. Instead his reply is both direct and discourteous. They are wrong because they know neither the Scriptures nor the power of God. Those who rise from the dead do not get married because they are like angels. Luke's version fills us in on this argument:

> The children of this world marry, and are given in marriage: but they which shall be accounted worthy to obtain that world, and the resurrection from the dead, neither marry nor are given in marriage: neither can they die any more for they are equal unto the angels and are the children of God being the children of the resurrection. (Luke 20:34–36)

This means that marrying and giving in marriage are realities proper to a world of death. For those for whom death is not a reality, marriage has no reason why. The impetus for procreation is the overcoming of death, and those who have nothing to do with death have no special motive for having children. God can create more beings in the same way as he creates angels: without any need for human reproduction.

This is Jesus' reply to the Sadducees' conundrum: having children is a necessity only for those who are dominated by death. For those who are not, it couldn't be less important. But his major premise is still to come. When he told the Sadducees that they understood neither the Scriptures nor the power of God, he dealt first with the Scriptures, by taking away their use of the example of the levirate law as valid evidence. But his major premise, which shows what he really thinks, is still to come: it is that of the power of God.

He doesn't run away from the Sadducees' premise — that God is only really understood from the Pentateuch — but answers with a quotation from the book of Exodus, itself in the Pentateuch. His quotation really doesn't seem to be an adequate reply, since it has nothing to do with the resurrection of the dead:

> I am the God of Abraham, and the God of Isaac, and the God
> of Jacob. (Luke 20:37 quoting Exodus 3:6, 15, 16)

The reply has no apparent bearing on the resurrection of the dead,
but rather is about who God is. God has nothing to do with death
nor with the dead, but instead declares to Moses that he is the God
of three people who were apparently dead at the time.

So when, earlier, Jesus had said to the Sadducees that they didn't
understand the power of God (*Tén dunamin tou theou*), now we begin to understand what this power might consist in. Jesus isn't talking
about some special power to do something miraculous, like raising
someone from the dead. Rather he's giving an indication of the sort
of power which characterizes God, something of the quality of who
God is. This "power," this quality which God always is, is that of
being completely and entirely alive, living without any reference to
death. There is no death in God. God has nothing to do with death,
and for that reason facts which are obvious to us, like Abraham,
Isaac, and Jacob having been long dead at the time of Moses, simply do not exist for God. Let's put this another way: for us "being
alive" means "not being dead"; it's a reality which is circumscribed
by its opposite. For God this is simply not the case. For God being
alive has nothing to do with death and cannot even be contrasted
with death.

I suggest that we have here something of great importance. Jesus
was able to imagine God, to perceive God, in such a way that his
whole vision was colored by God as radically alive, as a-mortal, as
in no way shaded by death. Those who started the dispute with him
were not able to perceive God in this way, and their theological arguments were, according to Jesus, vitiated from their roots. When Jesus
tells the Sadducees that they are greatly mistaken (*"poly planasthe"*),
he is not telling them that they have *made* a mistake, for example,
with respect to some detail, but that their whole perception is radically wrong, distorted, and it is so because it is stuck in a vision
which flows from death to death, a vision which has not acceded to
God, the entirely death-less.

We, of course, have certain advantages in comparison with Jesus'
first disciples when it comes to thinking about this. If you can imagine them present at the joust with the Sadducees you will place them,
of course, on Jesus' side. They would have rejoiced in his victory
over the Sadducees, congratulating themselves that their Master was
right and the Sadducees wrong. Of course, if you're on the winning

side, naturally you absorb some of the glory of the master's triumph against his adversaries. It is, then, much more difficult to understand that, in the light of Jesus' understanding it was not only the Sadducees who were mistaken about the point under discussion — the resurrection — but that in fact *being greatly mistaken in our whole perception of this world, including the things of God,* is part of the human condition. Our advantage over the disciples is that it is, perhaps, a little easier for us to understand that the same criticism meted out to the Sadducees applies to us.

It was really St. Paul who underlined this with all his strength. Unlike the disciples he was not under the impression that he was on Jesus' side in any argument. He well knew himself to have been on the other side: to have been involved in the persecution of Jesus and his way. He therefore knew very well that "you are greatly mistaken" is not just something which some people are, some of the time, but something we all are, all of the time, and that the fatal secret at the heart of our being in error is our need to kill, to persecute, to purify and cleanse in order to maintain security and order. So he writes in the first chapter of his epistle to the Romans, in what is one of the most powerful critiques of who we humans are to be found in literature, that we have all become futile (*emataiōthésan*) in our thought, that our senseless hearts (*asunetos kardía*) have darkened. Furthermore, *since* we will not recognize God, God has handed us over to a reprobate mind (*adokimon noun*) and an improper conduct. It is not just some people who are like this (and the use of this passage to fire off at some people rather than others is surely one of the great ironies of Christian history), but all of us. As Paul affirms at the beginning of what we know (but he didn't) as chapter 2, whoever dares to judge another judges himself or herself, since she or he does exactly the same. That is to say: the act of condemning someone else is absolutely part of the futile mind and the senseless heart.

According to Paul we are all challenged by the phrase which Jesus spoke to the Sadducees. It is spoken to all, since we are all in error with relation to God, with relation to the living power, the strength, vitality, and splendor of God. In fact, and here is a substantial point, the nucleus of the Gospel is no more than this: the announcement of the good news concerning *God.* What Jesus came to tell us, and to make possible for us to believe, was that God is entirely different from what we imagine. If by chance you should think I'm making this up, it is the view of a witness to the tradition as ancient as

Saint Ireneus,[1] so it is not such a strange thing to say as it sounds. What does it mean? It means that the good news is not, in the first place, the good news about Jesus, nor even about the resurrection, and certainly not primarily some sort of announcement about how we should behave ourselves. It is a novelty about God: who God is, how God is. Its starting point is that we are, all, in practice, incapable of perceiving how God is, not because we're stupid, but because our minds and imaginations are all darkened, senseless, and futile. Furthermore, it is in the degree to which we come to perceive how God really is, and to offer him service, that we will be able to alter our behavior to something more appropriate. Notice the order here: it is not that *if* we behave ourselves well, *then* we will be able to see God with clarity, but exactly the other way round. Insofar as we begin to have our minds changed by the good news about who God is, to that degree will we be able to behave ourselves in a human way. This distinction will become important for us in the chapters which follow.

Now please notice something rather special here, and I emphasize this because for much contemporary theology and exegesis what I'm going to say might seem inconceivable. Jesus was able to answer the Sadducees in the way he did because *his* imagination and heart were not darkened, senseless, futile. That is to say, he did not share the condition of the human heart in which, according to St. Paul, we all share. This was not because he was not human, nor because he was God instead of being human, but because his fully human imagination was capable of being fixed on the ineffable effervescence and vivacity, power and deathlessness of God in a way which seems almost unimaginable to us.

Here we are talking about something worthy of note: that Jesus had this extraordinary imagination *before* his passion and death; it was in fact this that was at work during his teaching about God. Of course the disciples couldn't understand fully what empowered Jesus to teach in this way, much less the signs which he worked, until after his resurrection from the dead. But when Jesus had risen they *could* begin to understand "the mind that was in Christ" (cf. 1 Cor. 2:16), his imaginative perception of God entirely without any of the sort of shading off into futility that death produces in us.

Now it is my claim that what we have in the New Testament, which is the apostolic witness put into writing, is the evidence of the

---

1. J. Ratzinger, *Teoría de los principios teológicos* (Barcelona: Herder, 1985), 19–20.

change in imagination which was produced in the disciples as they began to leave behind the "futile mind" and "senseless heart" proper to those whose vision is bound about by death, and as they began to be possessed by the same imaginative perception of the deathlessness of God that had been at work in Jesus. This is, in fact, a huge change, which occurred in their case, as it may in ours, very slowly, since it is the whole of human cultural perception which is being altered. So we are going to examine quite closely some of the changes of vision which come about in the degree to which it becomes clear that God is entirely without any relation to death: that death is for God something that is not.

The First Step: God Pruned of Violence

In the next chapter we're going to look at the way in which Jesus was himself empowered by his own imagination being centered on the completely deathless effervescence of God. However, for now suffice it to say that, thanks to his imagination fixed on God, Jesus was able to move *toward* death without being moved *by* death, or, as the epistle to the Hebrews describes it, in a quotation which I hope will become familiar to you:

> for the joy that was set before him, he bore the cross, despising the shame. . . . (Heb. 12:2)

This was not, of course, something that the disciples could begin to understand while they were accompanying him, since death was for them, as it normally is for all of us until we begin to understand the Gospel, the definitive stumbling block.

Let us try to imagine what this means in terms of the imagination which we normally have with relation to God. If your mind is absolutely quickened by the effervescent vivacity of God, then you can speak the sort of truth and reveal the sort of injustice which may well provoke people into killing you, since for you, unlike for them, truth is not decided by the survivors, or the victors, but could well be what it was claimed to be by the one who was killed. This, of course, can simply not be understood at all by those who do not share your perception of God. Their angle onto God still perceives him as in some way involved in death, for example by punishing or rewarding people with misfortune or success. So, if you are killed by a group of people, then it must have been God's will, and what you did and who you were has to be defined from your final failure: if Jesus died as a transgressor, then it must be because a transgressor he was. That means that what God thinks of you is a function of what the humans who have brought you to your end think of you. God is completely involved in violence: it is human hands which carry out God's murders.

If, on the other hand, God has nothing to do with death, then death is only a purely human cultural reality and no reflection of what you did and who you were. This means that what is good is in no way defined by death, and you are free to act in a way which doesn't respect the limits of good and evil which are imposed by living in the shadow of death. Now try to imagine the kind of shock which befalls those who are entirely bound in by death and whose vision of God has not been freed from shading into death when someone who was killed under the system of death, apparently punished by God, and certainly considered to have been the purveyor of a falsified vision of God, suddenly appears again, beyond death.

If we begin to imagine this shock, then we'll have done almost all the work which is proper to Christians who do theology or who try to understand God to some degree. For this is exactly what happened to the disciples at the resurrection of Jesus. God's whole project, including the deliberate mime and *mise-en-scène* of the undoing of death, was possible because Jesus was working out of an imagination which was simply not tinged by death, so that he could work beyond it. The first thing, then, which happened to the disciples as they began to understand was the complete shake-up of their vision of God. They began to be possessed by a totally different perception of God, the perception which Jesus had had during his life.

In the first place this change of perception meant that God was indeed as Jesus had claimed: brilliantly alive and completely without reference to death. It also meant that all other human attempts to describe or define God are wrong, and that every form of moral life is inadequate, because it doesn't go beyond death.

It is very difficult for us to imagine the huge change of perception underway here, but it could be described as the change from a perception of a god in which the deity has a double face, saying "yes, but..." or "yes, and no," or "yes, if...," to the perception according to which God only and unconditionally says "yes." Another way of putting it is as a change from a god who is both good and bad, who loves and who punishes, to a perception of God who is only love, in whom there is no darkness at all. Jesus had begun to teach this to his disciples, but it had been incomprehensible to them until after the resurrection. Consider Jesus' teaching that God makes the sun to shine on good and bad alike and causes the rain to fall on both the just and the unjust. This has the effect of removing God completely from the sphere of reference of our human morality, excluding him from any participation in judging and condemning humans. The same thing happens in the parables: we are not to separate the wheat from the tares (Matt. 13:24–30) in this life, because we cannot judge adequately, and God's judgment has nothing to do with our own. The same with the parable of the fish caught in the net (Matt. 13:47–50). Exactly the same point occurs in Luke 13:1–5: there is no link between any type of physical happening or accidental death and God's action, but those who think that there is are trapped in an understanding of God which is meshed in by death, and they had better repent or they too will perish.

Perhaps the matter was most clearly seen by Paul, as a result of his conversion. He had persecuted someone who, as he saw it, was leading people astray (causing them to err — *planaō*) from the God who had been revealed in the Law given to Moses. This man had been executed under the Law for leading people astray. At his conversion Paul perceived that, in fact, God really had raised this man up, and that he, Saul, was persecuting him in the name of God's Law, which meant that Jesus had been right about who God is, and furthermore the Law, and Saul's zeal for it, far from being a reflection of and a service to God, were instruments of death. Let's put it this way: on the one hand God is known and served in the service of the Law, which means that by persecuting and killing those whom the Law excludes, you are doing God's will and serving him. This means what we have seen: that God is loving kindness to the insiders, the obedient ones, and terrible in his punishments with the outsiders, those who sin and do not know the Law. Or, on the other hand, there is no ambivalence at all in God: God is not "love, but also vengeful justice," but purely and unambiguously love. In this case God does not know the Law, which may have been intended to teach people to be like God, but had become a purely human way of separating people and an instrument of death (a notion very well captured in John's Gospel, in the scene where the crowd shouts out to Pilate: "We have a law, and by that law this man must die" [John 19:7]). That is to say: Paul's conversion was from sharing the Ayatollah's view of God to sharing Jesus' view of the good shepherd, and it happened in the degree to which his perception of God was reformed starting from the victim whom we cast out.

The presence among the apostolic group of the risen victim thus served simultaneously to reveal that there is no violence in God and to unmask the violence that there is among humans. We could go through this process in detail, but then we'd never get to some properly eschatological questions, so we are going to look quickly at two "moments" in the change of perception. We will begin with a rather late moment of the process to which the New Testament bears witness, and then, in its light, we will move back to a previous moment, which will become clearer for us.

The later moment in the process is pretty evident, since it is as the process advances that it becomes possible to see what has been going on the whole time. Let us take the prologue to John's Gospel. It begins with a reference to the beginning of Genesis and to creation. You will remember that the story of creation is also the story of how we humans were expelled by God from paradise. The portrayal of God is ambiguous: God says "eat" and "do not eat," that is: "do" and "do not." The result is that we humans are expelled from Eden, and God is, in some degree, responsible for this expulsion. That's to simplify the matter a great deal, since in fact the story of Adam and Eve and their expulsion already marks a huge step toward the understanding of human responsibility for human acts. However, the story is completely demythologized in the prologue of John's Gospel. There it is not God who expels human beings from paradise, but we humans who expel God. The prologue is organized in the form of a chiasm (that is, with the verses arranged in a concentric pattern, usually in the form a-b-c-b'-a'). The culminating verse is thus the central one:

> He came unto his own, and his own received him not.
>
> (John 1:11)

God has nothing to do with the expulsion. That is a simply human mechanism: it is God whom we expel.

The Second Step: The Revelation of God as Love

It is not only that the living God is pruned of violence, by an act of negative theology, as it were. There is much more. In John 3:16 we can read a real step forward:

For God so loved the world that he gave his only begotten Son, that whosoever believeth in him should not perish, but have everlasting life.

This means that the apostolic meditation about the utterly living God revealed by Jesus and his resurrection had been able to reconsider what had been going on in Jesus' death. If we look at that death in the light of the violent god, we see a blasphemer who is killed to satisfy the law of god that whoever acts thus must die. However, if God raises up this man, then the first step is to recognize that the violence against that man was human and not divine — the separation of God from violence. The second step is to see that the disposition of that man to allow himself to be killed was not accidental, but a deliberate plan of self-giving to make it possible for us to *believe* in the utter vivacity of God, and thus to begin to live, ourselves, outside the dominion of death. That is to say, we can see a positive intention of love in the way in which Jesus gave himself up to death; and that positive intention of love is described by saying that God gave his only Son.

Now, this "giving his only Son" is not an idea pulled out of a hat. It is, itself, the demythologization of a story from the Old Testament: the story of Abraham who was prepared to give up his only (legitimate) son to God by sacrificing him. But look at what has happened meanwhile: in the first story God is a god who demands sacrifices from humans, including the one sacrifice which really mattered, even though, in the story as we have it in Genesis 22, God himself organizes a substitute for the sacrifice. In any case, we still have a capricious deity. What we see in the New Testament, completely in line with the change in the perception of God that I've been setting out, is that it is not humans who offer a sacrifice to God (by, for instance, killing a blasphemous transgressor), but *God who offers a sacrifice to humans*. The whole self-giving of Jesus becomes possible because Jesus is obedient to God, giving himself in the midst of violent humans who demand blood, in order finally to unmask and annul the system of murderous mendacity which the world is.

Once more, if you think I'm making this up, everything which I have been saying is beautifully and exactly resumed in the first epistle of John. There we see what the message is, the nucleus of the Gospel:

This then is the message which we have heard of him [i.e., Jesus], and declare unto you, that God is light and in him is no darkness at all. (1 John 1:5)

That is: what Jesus came to announce was a message about God and God's being entirely without violence, darkness, duplicity, ambivalence, or ambiguity. This message is then unpacked by the author in the following verses, and then he gives us the famous summing up of where this process of the changing perception of God has led to:

> ...for God is love. In this was manifested the love of God toward us, that God sent his only begotten Son into the world that we might live through him. Herein is love, not that we loved God, but that he loved us, and sent his Son to be the propitiation for our sins. (1 John 4:8–10)

Here we have the element of the discovery of the absolutely vivacious and effervescent nature of God leading to the realization that behind the death of Jesus there was no violent God, but a loving God who was planning a way to get us out of our violent and sinful life. Not a human sacrifice to God, but God's sacrifice to humans.

John illustrates the process pretty clearly, but somehow I'm making it easier for myself by jumping directly to the end of the process, skipping over some of the more difficult passages in, for example, the Pauline writings. So we'll take a quick glance at some of those, especially from the early stages in the process of demythologization, within which process the Pauline language is situated.

In the first place, Paul is pretty clear that the central message is that of the good news with respect to Who God is, God's absolute lack of ambiguity. To this he refers when he says at the beginning of Romans (1:17) that the Gospel reveals that God is righteous. He continues by pointing out that the effect of this revelation of the goodness of God is simultaneously to make apparent the injustice of humans, who by their injustice keep truth a prisoner to injustice, and this is described as the wrath of God. That is: the wrath of God is not understood as something which God does actively, but is rather the condition of human involvement in the murderous lie, which John also underlines. In case this is not grasped, it is worth remembering that Paul understands that to talk of the wrath of God in an active sense is merely a human way of speaking (cf. Rom. 3:5), whose real content is purely human. On all the other occasions that the term "wrath" appears in his writings, it appears as the impersonal term "the wrath," and not the wrath of God.[2]

---

2. The translators of the RSV have personalized *orgé*, wrath, wherever possible, with no textual justification.

The content of this wrath is, as I have suggested, purely human. God is described as handing us over to ourselves: this is the content of the wrath. But this term *paredoken* — (he) handed over — is very important in early Christian discourse, since the only really important handing over which took place was God's handing over of Jesus to us. In Romans 4:25 we are told that God handed over Jesus, and once again in Romans 8:32. That is to say it is God's handing over of Jesus to us which defines what "the wrath" is: the wrath is the type of world in which Jesus was borne to death by sinful humans who could not receive the truth. It is the giving, the divine handing over of the Son which reveals what the wrath is. This somewhat difficult argument becomes a little clearer if we remember what lies behind Romans 8:32:

> He that spared not his own Son, but delivered him up for us all ...

Many commentators imagine this to be a reference to the story of the sacrifice of Isaac, which we saw when we were looking at John. However, there the key word is *only begotten,* where here the key word is his own Son, as though there were some possibility that he might hand over someone else's son. In fact there is a passage in the Old Testament which has precisely to do with the handing over of someone else's son.[3] It is found at 2 Samuel 21. David discovers that the cause of a famine was Saul's murder of some Gibeonites, for which their relatives require a blood revenge. So David asks the Gibeonites what it is that they want to satisfy their just demand for vengeance. They demand that seven sons of Saul be handed over to them so that they may hang them up before the Lord, and David hands them over. That is: David was able to satisfy the anger of the Gibeonites by handing over *somebody else's* sons. The comparison with Romans is exact: God is not like David, who handed over someone else's sons to the Gibeonites to satisfy their wrath. God handed over his *own* Son, in this way forever revealing his goodness and generosity. Once again the notion of sacrifice is inverted: it is God who sacrifices to us, and we who demand sacrifice, not vice versa.

The purpose of this discussion is to demonstrate an earlier moment in the same process which we saw in John. Let us not imagine that

---

3. Here I would like to acknowledge my debt for Robert Hamerton-Kelly's exposition of this text in *Sacred Violence: Paul's Hermeneutic of the Cross* (Minneapolis: Augsburg Fortress, 1992), 78–79.

this process was easy. Paul, like the good Pharisee which he was, had an immense respect for the truth of the Scriptures in which he had been educated. He could not throw out without further ado a whole style of discourse about God. What we see instead is the slow way in which irony subverts the meaning of words from within. It works something like this: the first step, as is proper to any profoundly conservative religious tradition, is the maintenance of the language of the tradition, but giving it a different sense by means of an ironic juxtaposition, which is what we see here. When it becomes clearer what this means, there is a move to the second step, which is to let that language fall away altogether. This is the process we see in Paul and then in John. First language is kept and made ironic. Then when this language can be abandoned without fear of scandalizing people, it is replaced by a new, simple and positive, discourse. So, God's wrath, a real concept in the Old Testament, becomes God's wrath, an ironic concept whose content is purely human violence, and then this is reduced to "the wrath" by itself. Finally the language is abandoned as it becomes clear that violence is always and only human, and that God has nothing to do with it, and so we end up with the sort of language we see in the Johannine texts.

It is worthwhile stopping to consider what we've just said, since if we don't, we'll skate too lightly over an important point. John says that God is love, and we all parrot this somewhat easily, which leads to no end of banalities and flights of sentimentalism in our approach to matters religious, except when we become all serious and moralistic and remember that God is just, and punishes, and so on, so we expel and punish as if the Gospel had never been preached. Well, it's not like that. The phrase "God is love" is not one more slogan which we can tack on to the end of other things we know about God and which we can brandish when we feel like it. It is the end result of a process of human discovery which constitutes a slow and complete subversion from within of any other perception of God. That God is love is a certainty achieved in the degree to which it came to be discovered that God has nothing to do with human violence and death, and as it became clear that God has so little to do with those things that he was capable of subverting them through Jesus' being expelled as a sinner to show that the goodness and justice of God have nothing to do with our fatal and expulsive notions of goodness and justice. The perception that God is love has a specific content which is absolutely incompatible with any perception of God as involved in violence, separation, anger, or exclusion.

The Third Step: Creation in Christ

Thus far we have God as brilliantly alive, totally without violence, in no way circumscribed by death, who has revealed himself as loving humanity by giving himself to us to allow us to live outside, and beyond, the culture of death. However, by means of the same process a further dimension of God is revealed to which we will dedicate ourselves now. This is the understanding of God as Creator.

We are used to speaking about creation and salvation as if these were two rather different things. A scheme which crops up pretty frequently goes like this: first there was creation, something which happened at the beginning; then there was the "fall," however that may have taken place, in which we fell into a state from which we needed someone to rescue us; then God sent Jesus to save the situation, and now, even though it seems that in reality nothing has been saved, we know that it has been, and we hope for heaven. Let us look at some of the elements of this model, which seems to be the story that's in the background of both Catholic and Protestant orthodoxy. The first element which I want to bring out is that in this scheme the relationship between our present state and heaven is pretty distant; that is to say, it doesn't look as though Jesus has made much difference, so we sit and wait, getting involved in immensely complicated moral struggles, hoping that finally we'll be acceptable for heaven.

In the long run this model deserves the sort of criticism which it has in fact received, which is that it does nothing to encourage people to take seriously the things they might do to improve this life for themselves and others, except in the most superficial way, treating the symptoms and not the causes by means of works of charity and so on. The result of this has been the various movements, especially in the last century, though lasting well into this century, to reinterpret Christianity in terms of participation in a social progress toward a utopia, whether these movements have called themselves religious or not (and they have often conceived of themselves in fundamentally anti-religious terms). The problem is that the model "creation-fall-redemption-heaven" is much more powerful than it seems, and those who have rebelled against its explicitly religious form have found themselves, far too often, living out an even more cruel and distorted version of the same thing.

I don't think that the problem with this model is to be found in the relationship between "redemption" and "heaven," which is where the fighting has gone on, but in the relationship between creation and redemption. That is, the problem resides in the vision of creation and salvation as two different sorts of thing. First there was creation, an initial movement on the part of God; then there was salvation, a sort of rescue operation, in reality a very different sort of thing, with only the most tenuous of relationships with what went before. There is a great deal of difference between a factory, where cars are made out of raw matter, and a mechanic's garage, where they are repaired when they break down. The operations are of a different nature. Well, if creation and salvation are two different sorts of thing, it is not at all clear that there is a real relationship between the Creator and the Savior; or, in other words, it's not clear what God has to do with Jesus.

Now we have traces in the New Testament that this matter was considered by the apostolic group. That is to say, there are indications that the apostolic witnesses did indeed perceive that there is a clear relation between God the Creator and Jesus the Savior, and that to anchor oneself in saying that God so loved the world that he sent his only Son to save it *was not sufficient*. That revealed God as love, indeed, but it didn't show how that love had anything to do with God as Creator. The sort of God who sends someone to save someone might be like the worried father who rescues his child, or some treasure, from something over which he has no real control, like a burning skyscraper, or a sinking ship, something for which he is not really responsible.

The hints that we have that the apostolic group understood that this model was inadequate for the experience of God which they had, starting from the presence to them of the risen Jesus, are found in those passages which involve Jesus directly in creation. These are the passages which deal with the so-called "pre-existence of Christ." The most famous is John 1:1–3:

> In the beginning was the word, and the word was with God, and the word was God. The same was in the beginning with God. All things were made by him and without him was not anything made that was made.

Then there is Hebrews 1:1–3:

> God, who at sundry times and in divers manners spake in time past unto the fathers by the prophets, hath in these last days spoken unto us by his Son, whom he hath appointed heir of all things, by whom also he made the worlds; Who being the

brightness of his glory and the express image of his person, and upholding all things by the word of his power. . . .

Then three texts from the Pauline writings. First 1 Corinthians 8:6:

> But to us there is but one God, the Father, of whom are all things, and we in him; and one Lord Jesus Christ, by whom are all things, and we by him.

Then there are the longer hymns, probably composed before the Pauline letters, which are thought to be very early indeed, and because of this especially valuable in their witness to the understanding of the apostolic group after the resurrection. From these hymns I'll give the example of Colossians 1:13–20, which includes this:

> He is the image of the invisible God, the firstborn of all creation, for through him were created all things in heaven and on earth, visible and invisible, thrones, dominations, principalities and powers, all things were created by him and for him.

Here is my question: what was it that enabled the apostolic witnesses to link together Jesus and creation in this way? That is, to link creation and salvation in such a way that they come to be seen as the same thing? They are not asking a question about this, but merely affirming it, simply and triumphantly, about the Jesus whom they had known: that he was in some way intimately involved in creation itself. If we can find out what it was which they perceived to be the inner dynamic between creation and salvation, which enabled them to write verses like the ones we've read, then we'll be in a position to understand something of the third dimension of the change in the perception of God that I've been trying to set out. We'll also be in a much better position to understand the relationship between this life and heaven than we would be if we were to stay within the boring old arguments of the "creation-fall-redemption-heaven" model of understanding.

What I'm going to suggest now is new, and somewhat experimental, but, since it seems to fit in with the data of the apostolic witness, I'm going to risk it, and we'll see if it takes us forward at all. My suggestion is that Jesus' resurrection not only altered the perception of God by removing any last remnant of violence and by allowing God to be understood as unambiguously loving of humanity, but it also produced a change in the understanding of God as Creator. Please allow me to get to this by means of an example of what I think to be wrong. This is the notion that belief in the Creator was simply part of the Jewish inheritance shared in by Jesus and the apostolic group, without any need of alteration, since it was already firmly in place. Jesus then, wouldn't have made much difference, in any real sense, to the understanding of what it means to call God "Creator." He'd just have added "salvation" to a pre-existing notion of God, so that God was both Creator and then, a little later, Savior. Later on the apostles, through some sort of Christian apologetic trick, tacked on to the idea of creation the somewhat mythic-sounding notion that Jesus was involved in creation.

Instead of this I'm going to suggest something different, which puts the element of myth in its proper place. It is precisely the idea of creation in Christ which produces the final demythologization of the idea of creation. Now it is central to my approach that it be understood that the human perception of God as Creator is some-thing which, itself, has a history and is by no means a simple concept. Furthermore, Jesus, through his life, death, and resurrection didn't leave a received notion of God as Creator where he had found it, but worked the final change in the perception of God as Creator that had been developing throughout, and thanks to, the story of Jewish fidelity to God during their history. This we can glimpse as we look at the development of the perception of God as Creator. Of course, there are many accounts in different religions and cultures of a god, or gods, who create. What they do, in one way or another, is to sep-arate out elements starting from an original chaos, and then produce the plants, animals, and birds necessary for human subsistence. What they do seems beneficent to humans, for they implant order. There are traces of such a vision in the story of the creation in Genesis, where God appears creating not from nothing, but from an initial chaos which needs to be ordered.

This means that the god in question is responsible not so much for creating everything out of nothing as for producing the order of the world. This means that the god is tied to the order of the world, and the order of the world is a reflection of the god. However, we have just seen that one of the things which the resurrection did was to sep-arate God from any link with the order of this world, which came to be understood to be a violent order, founded on death. In the Jew-ish tradition the development of the perception of God as Creator was not something rapid or sudden. The chosen people first had to move from a view which saw God as one among many gods, merely more important and powerful, to another according to which God was the only God, Creator of all things, including the enemies of Israel. It is possible that this intuition came to be firmly established only as a result of the Babylonian exile, that is, as a result of the apparent defeat of God by the Babylonic deities. We are talking about the movement from polytheism to monolatry to monotheism. However, the perception that God created everything is not the same as the perception that God created everything *out of nothing*. That perception was reached later, in the same period as the resurrection of the dead came to be understood.

Now it is very important that these two beliefs should have developed at the same time and are apparently related. The principal evidence for this is in the text of 2 Maccabees. There it is understood that God has to raise from the dead those who have been so loyal to him that they have allowed themselves to be killed out of faithfulness to his Law. This was what happened to the Maccabee brothers. That is to say, it was inconceivable that God, having given his Law, should deal with those who were prepared to die rather than disobey it in the same way as their executioners. But it also means something fundamental: that the order of this world does *not* correspond to God's order, since those who obey God are persecuted in this world. So God's order has to be of a different nature than the order of this world; it has to be an order of which God's law is a reflection and which cannot be easily lived in this world because of persecution. The perception that God raises those who died out of loyalty to the Law is thus a perception which allows a small but vital separation between God and the order of this world. God as Creator is not responsible for the order of this world, which turns out to be frequently contrary to the divine will. The establishment of order out of chaos is the work of human violence, and creation is prior to this and not party to it, since those who obey the Creator suffer the consequences of this ordering violence.

It was the persecution of the Maccabee brothers, innocent because of their fidelity to God, that simultaneously opened two cracks in the old perception of God: the first crack is that there must be a resurrection life for those whom God loves, since God's life cannot be limited to the prizes bestowed in this life, for in this life the just are killed; the second crack is that if God is to be understood as Creator, then that understanding cannot remain bound to the maintenance of the order of the world, which is not a reflection of God. In other words, God's graciousness which raises up those whom God loves is the same graciousness as that which brings into being out of nothing. Because of this the mother of the Maccabees says:

> My son, I beg you, look at the heaven and the earth, look at all they contain and you will see that God created it all out of nothing, and humans have the same origin. Do not fear this executioner, do not let your brothers down, but accept death. In this way through God's mercy I will receive you back along with them. (2 Macc. 7:28–29)

In the case of the Maccabees, this was still seen within a partial and moralizing vision of God. God created the world and would give back life to those who were persecuted on his account. That is to say, resurrection is a form of eschatological revenge, a post-mortem triumph, over the persecuting enemies, in the same way that creation happened to bring Israel to existence. We are still in the world of the partial: the perception of God still has to be filled out.

I hope that this has made clearer the correction which Jesus' resurrection made to this introduction of cracks into an image of God that was too bound to this world. It is important to notice that this correction was also made in the overcoming of a case of persecution, as with the Maccabees, but this time with certain differences. In this case it could not be affirmed that the persecution was carried out by a special group of iniquitous people, foreign to the chosen people of God. No, it was rather an indiscriminate mix of the chosen people and the representatives of the gentiles which put Jesus to death, each side for its own reasons, which were, in fact, no reason at all: *They hated me without a cause.*

The resurrection revealed that persecution was not the monopoly of any particular group, but is the logical result of the fact that all of humanity is locked into a certain sort of blind and murderous violence, no bit of it more or less than others. That this should have happened in the midst of the chosen people doesn't mean that they were especially iniquitous, as a grotesque Christian discourse about "the people who killed God" has far too often had it, but merely, and sadly, that they, the best of the nations of the earth, were also locked into the same mechanism of violence which flows from death to death.

We have seen that Jesus knew from the beginning what he was doing, completely possessed as he was by his quickened imagination of the ever-living God. It was this which enabled him to stage a solemn mime in the midst of this death-based culture, so that he might be killed as a way of leading people out of that culture based on death, allowing us to come to be what God always wanted us to be, that is, utterly and absolutely alive with him. What Jesus' entirely living imagination means, then, is that he was working to bring to existence what God had always wanted, but which had become trapped in the violent and fatal parody which we have seen, and which we tend to live out. So what Jesus was bringing into being was the fulfillment of creation, and this he knew very well as he was doing it. We will look in the next chapter at one of the most remarkable passages in Scripture, in which John portrays Jesus doing exactly this, with full knowledge of what he was doing.

This means something rather important: the understanding of God as Creator changes from someone who once did something to someone who is doing something through Jesus, who was in on what the Father was doing through him from the beginning. Creation is not finished until Jesus dies (shouting *tetelestai* — it is accomplished), thus opening the whole of creation, which consequently begins fully, in a completely new way, in the garden on the first day of the week. This means, and here is the central point: we understand creation starting from and through Jesus. God's graciousness, which brings what is not into existence from nothing, is exactly the same thing as Jesus' death-less self-giving out of love which enables him to break the human culture of death and is a self-giving which is entirely fixed on bringing into being a radiantly living and exuberant culture. It is not as though creation were a different act, something which happened alongside the salvation worked by Jesus, but rather that the salvation which Jesus was working was, at the same time, the fulfillment of creation. This was the power and the authority in Jesus' works and words and signs. Through him the Creator was bringing his work to completion. The act of creation was revealed for what it really is: the bringing to existence and the making possible of a human living together which does not know death; and Jesus was in on this from the beginning. Such is our world that God could be properly perceived as Creator only by means of the overcoming of death.

I hope that you see what it means that our underlying model for understanding the Christian faith has changed slightly, but significantly. Rather than the "creation-fall-redemption-heaven" model, according to which we live between the redemption and heaven, the model is: "The redemption reveals creation by opening up its fulfillment in heaven and reveals at the same time the fall as that which we are in the process of leaving behind." This second approach respects the order of discovery, that is to say, the fact that all these realities were discovered at all only as a result of the life, death, and resurrection of Jesus.

Everything said up till now has been a long meditation on the change of imagination and perception worked in the apostolic group by the resurrection. If it seems hard to follow, it is because it is hard, demanding of us an effort to sustain a concentration on the utter effervescence of God which was revealed by Jesus. We've seen that the resurrection opened a new perception onto God: that God is entirely beyond, and has nothing to do with, death; that God has touched our murderous world with love, allowing us to break out of death; that this is what creation has been about from the beginning, and that Jesus, who knew all this, was thus the original man who was in on it all from the beginning. In the next chapter we'll look at how the apostolic witnesses came to perceive what we might call the inner dynamic which was at work in Jesus' life as he brought about this change of perception.

The Discovery of Jesus' Imagination

In our second chapter we examined the way in which the presence of the crucified and risen Lord among the apostolic group unleashed the process of the change in the perception of who God is.[1] In this way the apostolic group was able to remove any vestiges of violence from God, then understand God as love, and we saw finally how this led them to understand God as Creator. Our starting point was the examination of Jesus' own perception of the deathlessness and effervescence of God, as he let that be glimpsed in his discussion with the Sadducees. In this way we were able to begin to understand something of how the apostolic group began to understand how Jesus had, in fact, understood God, and his own relation with God before his death. Please notice that the process of working all this out was very slow, for there is no change in our perception of God without a corresponding change in our perception of ourselves and of our relationship with others. Just consider how long each one of us takes to leave behind a view of God that is dominated in some way by our own parents, and how much time passes before the change in relationships which this inspires is translated into practical changes in what we do, how we serve others, and so on.

What we will look at in this chapter is how, little by little, it came to be understood that Jesus himself had understood what he was about. Some of you will be used to more rationalist schools of exegesis, which tend to deny any possibility of our understanding what Jesus really thought or imagined that he was doing. If that is your case, it may well be that what follows will be painful to you, since my presuppositions are somewhat different. My starting point is that the author of John's Gospel (whom I will call John) considered it perfectly possible, although difficult, to set out Jesus' thought. Not

---

1. It may help readers to follow this chapter if they read John 14–16 beforehand, and then accompany their reading of this chapter with that Gospel close at hand.

only that, but he believed it possible to give us clear indications of what enabled Jesus to do what he was doing. You may remember that in the last chapter I suggested to you some signposts on the way to the discovery that God is love. Essential for this discovery is the apostolic group's perception, after the resurrection, that Jesus had not died by accident, but that he knew full well that he was going to be killed. In the synoptic Gospels he even refers to his death as *necessary*. What came to be understood was that Jesus' death was more than a painful necessity, since in it Jesus was no merely passive participant. There is a deliberate element in the way in which Jesus goes to his death, and this deliberate element has nothing to do with any masochism or death wish. Quite the contrary. It is the attitude of someone who is so entirely free of being involved in death that he manages to mount, to stage, a show, a mime, in such a way that other people will be able to learn to live as if death were not. That is the difference between dying and redeeming death. Someone who is totally and utterly free with respect to his death is capable of making of his death a sort of "show" which takes the sting out of death's tail, detoxifying the reality of death, revealing it to be without power, and doing this forever.

If we do not grasp this, we are not going fully to grasp how it could be understood that Jesus' death had anything to do with love. Let us take the phrase from John's Gospel which we have looked at: that God so loved the world that he gave his only-begotten Son. Now, how could God love *Jesus* if he gives him to be killed? Doesn't this seem to be a somewhat operatic plot? The sort of barbarous love in which the hero has to choose between losing the world or killing his son in order to save it? Well, that would be true if it were also true that Jesus was sent to be killed, just like that, as though the fact of Jesus' being killed of itself does any good to anybody.

The point is somewhat different. As it is understood that there is no violence in God and that the violence which was once attributed to God is purely human, it came to be understood that God had a project for the overcoming of violence and that that project was something about which Jesus was fully aware and in which he was the active human participant. The project was, if you'll excuse the inappropriate language, to organize a sort of stage death — a real death but transformed into theater[2] — from which he would rise, so as to

---

2. I was tempted to shy away from using the word "theater," for it seems to suggest something unreal, a mock performance. That is not at all what I mean: acting something out does not make it any less real, but rather more so. When people put on, or stage, a

reveal the impotence of death, and with it the impotence of all the mechanisms of violence which dominate our lives.

We know, because we followed Jesus when he was explaining it to the Sadducees, that Jesus understood full well that for God death is not, so that God's loving and sustaining of a person is not something which is interrupted or diminished by death. This means that Jesus was able to conduct his life in a way that was not moved by death. And this not because he was fleeing from death, or running toward it in a self-destructive way, which tend to be our problems. It was because it was not a reality which marked his imagination, since his imagination was entirely fixed on the creative and living presence of God who knows not death. What can be perceived by someone who is not marked by death is the way in which the rest of us live, without being aware of it, in the shadow of death. A poor parallel might be the way in which someone arriving from an Islamic country, in which there is no alcohol to buy or to consume, is able to perceive something which we scarcely realize: the degree to which our whole society and its social life depend on the dangerous drug, alcohol. Only those from outside can perceive that clearly. Only those who have not received their identity from a culture that is bound in by death can see clearly the way in which the whole culture is wrapped around by death. It is in this sense that Jesus was able to understand with perfect clarity the way that human culture, including the culture in which he lived, is produced by, and runs toward, death. It also means that he was aware that such a culture reacts to someone who isn't part of it, is not complicitous with it, who doesn't participate in the rules of the game of a security which runs from and toward death. Human culture reacts as if faced by a threat, expelling, and preferably killing, such a person.

So Jesus was able to see what was going to happen to him, not thanks to some prophetic gift in the sense of special, secret inside information about what was going to happen at the next step, but in the much more radical sense of the prophetic gift of one who, possessed by the life and vivaciousness of God, was able to understand

---

homecoming reception for someone, they are not pretending to receive that person; their staging really is their reception. Dramatization can be a way of making something real. If, to show my friends that I love them, I climb Mount Everest to pluck some special flower which they need that grows only there, the hardship and exertion involved in scaling the North Face is no less real for my whole action being my way of dramatizing my love for them, which is what makes that love really effective. To stage, to make a theater of, a dying in this sense does not in any way reduce the real human pain, grief, and horror of what is gone through.

exactly the workings of a culture shot through with death. Because of this he was able to go to his death as if it were not. And not only to go toward it as if it were not, but to make of it a show, a sign so that others might live in the same way.

When we speak, then, of God as love, it is not as if God loved us by throwing Jesus to us as if we were a pack of hungry crocodiles. No, God's love for us is the love by which Jesus was empowered *as a human being* to create for us — which means to understand and imagine and invent for us — a way out of our violence and death. There is a certain piety which imagines Jesus on the cross, with the Father observing from above. In some versions the Father is pleased, because he is being offered a sacrifice which will wipe out our sins; in another sort of piety the Father is horrified by the cruelty which we are showing toward his Son. Neither of these seems to me to be adequate. The Father was present at the cross not as a spectator, but as the source of the loving self-giving which was bringing into existence the possibility that we humans might overcome death and its dominion in our lives: God was not attending our show, but was busy in making of a typical show of ours a revelation of himself to us.

Now, having said this as a preface, let us look at how John understood the human and creative imagination that was in Jesus.

The Johannine Understanding of the Act of Believing

The first key to understanding John 14–16 is the fundamental importance of John's understanding of belief. Jesus' imagination is absolutely possessed by God's deathless vivaciousness. Ours is not. The access which we have to that deathless vivaciousness is by the slow opening of our imagination to that reality; that is what we understand by faith: the keeping open of our mind and imagination to the utter vivaciousness and deathlessness of God. So Jesus tells us:

Believe in God... (John 14:1)

Jesus knows that we cannot have our mind opened in this way by a mere instruction or explanation. We need a fully human illustration, a model, something which we can follow and do. So he exhorts us:

... believe also in me. (John 14:1)

Jesus' rôle has been to choose and sustain some people in whose presence he can act out, make humanly comprehensible, what it is to be a human whose mind is entirely possessed by the aliveness of God. It is their believing in Jesus, and thus their following what happens in what he is about to carry out, which will permit these witnesses to have their minds and imaginations possessed in the same way.

At the end of chapter 14 Jesus comes back to exactly the same point:

> I tell you this now, before it happens, so that when it happens, you may believe. (John 14:29)

He wants his witnesses to understand that what is about to happen to him is not accidental, but is part of what will allow them to come to understand the deathlessness of the Father. That is: he is going to his death *to create a belief.* A comparison might be that of the motorcycle instructor who, accelerating up a ramp in the presence of his pupils, jumps through a ring of flame held high over fifteen cars, and then lands on a ramp on the other side. His novice bikers had previously considered this impossible: fear of gravity and of fire had definitively held them back from trying it. Their instructor has produced in them a belief in him, in a way that they can imitate, and then they do the same as he. Well, this was what Jesus was doing: he was producing in his disciples a belief in the non-importance of death by passing through it himself in the first place to show that it is possible.

The De-celestialization (or Un-heavening) of Heaven

The next "moment" at which we must look is the way in which John understands Jesus to have "de-celestialized" heaven. This is the special meaning of the phrase "I go to my Father." It is part of John's theology that this phrase refers to two realities at the same time. Just as the cross in John is simultaneously the death of Jesus and his triumph (his lifting up or exaltation, mentioned in John 3:13–15 refers to both at the same time), in the same way his going to the Father means simultaneously his going to death and his going to heaven: for John the two "goings" are the same thing. It is in his dying that Jesus fulfills the work which the Father sent him to carry out, the bringing about of the possibility that we humans might live beyond death, so that it is as he dies that he cries out *tetelestai* — "it is accomplished" — saying by this that the divine creation has been brought to fulfillment in this his creative act of dying. So, when we hear the phrase "I go" in these chapters, let's try to alter our traditional frame of reference, which suggests that by this phrase Jesus meant that he was going to heaven. "I go" means "I am going freely, as a creative act, to my death, and it is in this that I go to the Father."[3]

So Jesus *is going* in order to prepare for us a place: it is his going to death which opens up for us the possibility of a place with the Father. It is his *going* which constitutes the only way to the Father, since apart from the creative and deliberate self-giving up to death of Jesus, there is no access, no way for us to begin to have our imaginations re-formed by the vivaciousness of God, and thus to begin to share actively in his life, *because we cannot, as we are, imagine beyond, or outside, our formation within death.* It is only by knowing Jesus and his self-giving that we begin to have any knowledge of the Father:

> If you had known me, you would also know my Father.
>
> (John 14:7)

Jesus also tells us that it is *thanks to the fact* that he is going to the Father that we will be able to do the works which he does and, indeed, greater works still. This does not mean that it is in Jesus' absence that we believers will be able to do these things, but that *thanks to* Jesus' creative self-giving up to death we will be able to be possessed by the Father in the same way in which Jesus was. In this way we can imitate him creatively, without rivalry, doing what he did and more. We can become involved in a non-rivalistic and creative imitation of Jesus. Jesus emphasizes this himself later when he says:

> It is expedient for you that I go, because if I do not go, the defense counsellor will not come to you; but if I go, I will send him to you. (John 16:7)

That is to say, it is the creative self-giving up to death which makes it possible that we be possessed by the same Spirit by which he was possessed, and so empowered to do the same things, and even more.

---

3. It is worth noticing that the word "heaven" doesn't appear in John 14–16 and appears only once in John 17, as a spatial indication (Jesus lifted up "his eyes to heaven").

However, please note what this means: it means that heaven is not just a place beyond death and that Jesus has to pass through the midst of death, so to speak, before we can be joined to him in heaven, which would be to miss the point of what he is saying. The meaning is that Jesus' going to death is *itself* the opening of heaven, and heaven will forever consist not of something which has simply left death behind and which has nothing to do with our present humanity. Heaven is a dwelling in the Father which is possible only for those for whom death has come to be a non-definitive, non-toxic part of their story. Once again we are face to face with the central mystery of the Christian faith, which is that Jesus the risen Lord is risen *as* crucified victim. Death is swallowed up by glory (cf. 1 Cor. 15:54).

Jesus' Creation of Divine Paternity for Us

If we begin with a general notion of God and understand that it so happened that Jesus called this God his Father, then we would have an image of someone who was insisting, rather pretentiously, that he had a special relationship with someone who is, in principle, equally accessible to all. This makes him rather like teacher's pet: someone rather despicable in the eyes of everyone else. Well, this is the inverse of what happens in the way in which Jesus speaks of "my Father" and says things like:

> no one comes to the Father but by me. (John 14:6)

Jesus starts from a completely different position: that there is no general notion of God that is in principle accessible to all, but that the available notions of God are pretty much false, and not only false, but also fatal. This position is amply illustrated in his discussion with some Jews who had believed in him in John 8, where he compares two different sorts of father: his Father and the father of his interlocutors. These notions of paternity are radically and incompatibly different: one notion is that of a father who, however unblemished his pedigree seems to be, in practice leads his children to lying and killing. Jesus links this father to the murder of Abel by Cain (John 8:44). We might call him the father of the founding murder; traditionally he is known as the devil, and the devil understood not as a mythical figure, red, with horns like the Greek god Pan, with a trident in his hand "all the better to roast you with," but that much more worrying figure, a satanized god, someone who seems to be God but is in fact an obstacle, an accusation, the whisperer behind the lynch. Jesus is saying, in reality, to his interlocutors: the God who has been revealing himself to Israel during all this time *is not* the one who you say; your interpretation and use of God turn him into Satan; only my interpretation of him is faithful to who God truly is.

Jesus affirms that his Father is unknown *and impossible to know* except through him, and not because he's being pretentious or teacher's pet, but because the secret of that satanized god is death: while people are still formed by a world which begins and ends in death they have no way of knowing a God who has nothing to do with death. Only someone who does not know death can begin to make accessible who that God is. So Jesus, at the same time as he makes possible *belief* in the utter vivaciousness of God, also *creates* the possibility of God's paternity among human beings. Before Jesus' self-giving it was effectively impossible that we be children of the Father, that is, moved from within by one who is self-giving love, because we were locked in to death. The possibility of coming to be children came about not through some general decree of adoption, but through a creative act that demanded a *mise-en-scène,* a particular human acting out.

I want to emphasize this once more: Jesus didn't come to tell us that God is our Father. That is excessively banal. He came to create the possibility that God in fact be our Father, or rather, that we should really become God's children, which is, in every case, something strictly impossible for humans to be naturally, since we are all enclosed in a mistaken identification of God with an ambiguous or satanic figure. This is what John understands when he talks of "the world," "the prince of this world," and so on. He is talking about life under the paternity of the murderous lie. If you read John 15:18–16:4 in this light, it may make more sense than before:

> the hour is coming when whoever kills you will think that they are offering a service to God, and this they will do because they have not known the Father nor me. (John 16:2–3)

There we have the two different sorts of paternity set out with absolute clarity: the paternity which kills and persecutes in order to serve "god," and the paternity which is shown in the self-giving in the midst of violence as a witness to the complete vivaciousness of the God who knows not death.

Now, this puts into question any universal notion of God, with respect to whom we can agree in polite conversations, with little phrases like: "after all, we're all God's children." Of which god are we children? This can be deduced from our practical behavior: the revelation of God's complete aliveness is the same thing as the making possible the practical living out of a way of bearing witness to that vivacity, the style of life of a witness, or, in Greek, a martyr, a style of life that is always prepared to run the risk of being expelled rather than participating in any human solidarity in expulsion. It seems important to emphasize this since, if we don't, we may have too familiar and domesticated a notion of God, which will make it difficult for us to wake up to the strangeness of the fact that it needed someone to die to make it possible for us to understand how different our real Father and Creator is. There is no access to him except from within that process of self-giving.

The Sending of the Holy Spirit

Jesus says to his disciples that he will ask the Father and the Father will give them another defense counsellor, someone other than Jesus, who will defend them against all accusation (John 14:16). A little later he says that the defense counsellor will be sent by the Father *in Jesus' name* (John 14:26). Then he tells them that *he himself* will send them this defense counsellor from the Father (John 15:26). And a little later he tells his disciples that:

> ...if I do not go, the defense counsellor will not come to you;
> however if I go, I will send him to you. (John 16:7)

Finally he tells them that when this Spirit comes, it will glorify Jesus, since it will take what is of Jesus and will declare it to them (John 16:14).

It seems pretty confused, especially if we're still stuck in our "celestialized" vision of the sending of the Holy Spirit: Jesus going up to heaven after his resurrection, and there negotiating some deal with his Father with respect to who sends the Spirit. Perhaps they could have a heavenly little fight to see who gets to do the honors: the Father by himself, or the Father through the Son, or the Father and the Son. While they're wasting their eternal time arguing divinely, we're no further on.

Of course, our passages have nothing to do with this. They have to do with something rather different. The idea seems to be as follows: Jesus, by going actively and deliberately to his death, opens up the possibility that his practice, his creative practice of self-giving, may come to be something which possesses others as well. His act of giving the Holy Spirit doesn't mean that he's sending to the world some sort of friendly numinous force, a consolation prize for his absence, but rather that *thanks* to what he is doing thus creatively, he has opened the possibility of a constantly repetitive re-creation of the same process. The Holy Spirit is the inner dynamic of what Jesus was doing, of his being sent by the Father and his acting in loving obedience to him. And, from the moment when the dominion of death, whose prince is the accusing god, has its lie revealed by Jesus living as if death were not, from that moment on it becomes infinitely and creatively possible that we be possessed by the same dynamic that was at work in Jesus, and so do the same as he, and greater things besides, *thanks to the fact that* he has gone to the Father.

However, this giving of the Holy Spirit is not an invisible, celestial event, which happens offstage, as we so often imagine. In reality it is a historical and creative staging, a visible acting out. The whole process by which Jesus went to his death as a real, historical, conscious act of subversion of violent human practice: that *was* the act of giving the Holy Spirit. All the Gospels without exception bear a subtle witness to this when they describe Jesus on the cross "giving up" his spirit, or "breathing out" his spirit, which is the same thing as his dying. That is, the Holy Spirit is given us as the possibility of re-creating the same witness to the Father, which means being a child of the Father by staging the same "show," with of course, infinite variations of circumstance. This is what it means when Jesus says:

> If they have persecuted me, the same will they do with you. If they kept my word, the same will they do with yours. But all of this they will do on account of my name, because they do not know the One who sent me. (John 15:20–21)

So Jesus is making possible as a normal human practice the infinitely creative dynamic of the continuous re-presentation of the passion. He is not doing this independently of other human people: his purpose is to make available the divine inner dynamic as a new human story in the midst of the usual human story of expulsion and death. One part of the sending of the Holy Spirit *is* the preparation of the witnesses and is the making possible texts which call to mind who Jesus was, and what he was doing. All this is part of what Jesus was doing when he sent the Holy Spirit: making accessible a new sort of human practice in the midst of the old one.

Let us now examine two elements of this new human practice: the Holy Spirit as defense counsellor and the Holy Spirit as the one who leads to the truth. The Holy Spirit as defense counsellor is not an accidental term. The word *Parakletos* is quite simply the forensic term. This attorney[4] exists to absolve people from any accusations against them. The opposite of the defense counsellor is the accuser, the counsellor for the prosecution, a euphemism for the word "persecution" from which it is derived. There we have, exactly in place, the double dynamic of mimetic theory: the counsellor for the persecution, representing the order of this world, justifies the need for the murder, the exclusion, and the expulsion in order to maintain order, social peace, in order to keep in check the violence within the group, and so on, and all this it does thinking that it is serving God (and perhaps today we might add "and America," or "the fatherland," or whatever). The defense counsellor reads the same lynch but from the point of view of the victim: it knows that the victim is hated without cause, and constantly declares the victim's innocence. It does this by constantly bringing to memory the real story, which happened historically, of the teaching and the works of Jesus, the original defense counsellor, the original forgiveness of God. Whatever may be the circumstances in which Jesus' followers find themselves, they need not fear: they will undergo the same treatment as he, and the same defense attorney will be on hand declaring their innocence, exposing the mechanism of the lie, and letting them off. This is the primordial function of the Holy Spirit, pleading for the defense, which corresponds exactly to the forgiveness of sins and the process of creatively producing children of God.

Please notice what this means: it means that the forgiveness of sins and the creative staging of the passion in the circumstances of the lives of the disciples of Jesus are the same thing. In the degree to which each one has their imagination possessed by the utter aliveness of God, in that same degree the cultural mechanisms by means of which we are moved in function of death become visible in us and are brought to our memories. But *they cease to be accusations against us;*

---

4. Those with an irremediably celestial vision of things may like to think of a sort of heavenly Perry Mason.

that is, whatever our future may be, it is no longer defined by these mechanisms, nor do they lock us in. This occurs exactly in the degree to which we are staging, acting out in a creative way, bringing into existence, a human practice which is non-accusatory, non-exclusive of others. It is this, I suspect, that Jesus means when he teaches us to forgive others so that we may be forgiven. As we come to be part of the real and creative acting out of the rôle of the defense against the lynch mechanisms of this world, in that same degree we find that our memories of what we have done wrong come to be simple descriptions of where we used to be and not accusations which seek to define us, condemning us to be forever according to what we have done.

The second point is linked to this: it is the defense counsel who will lead us into the whole truth (John 16:13). I hope that you now understand the underlying logic behind this declaration of Jesus. By "leading us into the whole truth" Jesus doesn't mean that the more we receive the Holy Spirit, the more we will advance in the knowledge of a whole series of arcane secrets which God has hidden in his bosom. Nor is it the guiding toward the truth which leads Sherlock Holmes to discover the real murderer who committed the crime (which is perhaps the most recurring model we have for the search for the truth, the forensic model, which seeks to blame someone for something). It is rather the reverse of these models: leading us into the whole truth means *the active and creative overcoming of the lie which is at the root of human culture,* leaving completely behind the recurrent fascination with that mendacious story. We've already seen what that lie means: it is the lie which says that the victim is guilty, and that by producing unanimity about this, we really are producing peace. The lie is produced by death and leads to death. It is creative of absolutely nothing at all. Jesus is clear when he tells his disciples:

> I still have many things to tell you, but you cannot bear them now. When the Spirit of truth comes, he will guide you into all truth.... He will take what is mine and declare it to you.
> (John 16:12, 13a, 14b)

The Spirit of truth makes constantly available the visible, creative, and historical act of Jesus' "going to his Father" as something which enables us to create the truth, as something new, fresh, beautiful, diverse, starting from the mendacious story of this world in which we all share.

The Creation of Meaning and the Forging of Love

There is a further point that I would like to touch on briefly here, tied to what I've tried to set out with respect to the sending of the Holy Spirit. It is about the way in which Jesus' active and creative practice is, so to speak, the active and creative bringing to being of what we might call an "open definition." This sounds like a contradiction, after all, definitions are instruments we use to close off meaning: the definition of a cow excludes the possibility that we are speaking about a sheep. An open definition, by contrast, would be a creative openness toward diversity of something which always starts from the same. We might call this a "flexible paradigm" or something like that. The point is this: Jesus' creative self-giving toward his death opened up for us the possibility that we might begin to inscribe ourselves in an immense variety of different and meaningful stories, all of which have as their starting point the creative human overcoming of death.

This seems to me to be tremendously important, because of the tendency which many of us have to reduce Christian life to a series of rules, whose ideal would be that we should all do and be the same. Jesus' imagination here in John 14–16 apparently works in an entirely different way: the monotony of rules and of similarity forms part of the expulsive order of death. But Jesus, by going to his Father, is making "many mansions" available. That is, he was able to imagine, his imagination was nourished by, a huge creativity in God, the type of immense creative diversity that we cannot imagine while our imaginations go round in death-bound cycles. This immense creative diversity is ours in the degree to which each of us permits the Father and the Son to make their dwelling in us. The word "dwelling," *moné,* appears at the beginning of chapter 14:

In my Father's house there are many dwellings. (John 14:2)

and then again at 14:23

The one who loves me will keep my word, and my Father will love him and we will both come to that one and make our dwelling with him.

The meaning is as follows: by going to his death, Jesus is creating the possibility that we should begin to create an entirely diverse story with our lives in the degree to which we are creatively empowered to overcome the story of death in the circumstances in which we live.

What we are given then is the possibility of creating, and of participating in, meaning. This is a story which is always different, yet is always the story of how we came to discover and live in the truth, as we learned to overcome the story of death and the many ways in which this story moves our lives with its compulsive repetitions and its infinite weariness.

I know that this is a rather difficult matter, but let us see how it is applied in the case of love. Jesus' single commandment, that we should love each other, is exactly what I have called an "open definition" or a flexible paradigm. Here it seems to me that we are frequently led astray by the banality of the use of the word "love." We often interpret Jesus' words about love from within a general notion which we have of love, that is, love is a general term embracing passion, affection, addiction, compulsion, generosity, sex, and other realities besides. According to a certain fairly widely held view, Jesus is talking about a special subsection of this general notion: the sort of love that requires sacrifice, especially so that someone else may live. This is commemorated especially in monuments to the fallen and other sacralized horrors, where people remember their companions, whose rush to the enemy lines, exposing themselves to risk and in fact taking them to their death, was "the greatest sacrifice."

Well, I beg to dissent, without in any way wishing to diminish the merits of the young men whose blood has built our universe, led on by what an English poet called:

the old lie: dulce et decorum est pro patria mori.[5]

Jesus is not talking about a particular subsection of the general term "love." Rather he is creating a new open definition of love. We could paraphrase John 14:23 as follows:

It is in allowing their imagination and practice to be expanded beyond the culture sunk in death in which they were born, by means of what I have taught and carried out, that people love me. Your loving me consists exactly in this. By doing this, the entirely living and creative self-giving of my Father will come to possess you, and the Father and I will make of you someone

---

5. "How sweet and fitting it is to die for one's country" (Horace, Odes 111.2).

who is an active, visible, historical participant in our creation of a story of a diversity which knows not death.

Jesus then emphasizes what I have called his open definition, his inauguration of an infinitely diverse flexible paradigm:

> This is my commandment: that you love one another as I have loved you. No one has greater love than this: that he should give his life for his friends. You are my friends if you do what I command you.

The commandment is that we should learn to imitate flexibly and creatively, doing the same thing as Jesus. Now please notice something which is generally not noticed on account of the infinitely sententious and solemn use to which these verses are put. Jesus gives us his open definition, his flexible paradigm of love as giving one's life for one's friends. By doing this, he is *not* making a solemn gesture of renunciation so that others may live. The words "for his friends" are immediately qualified in the following phrase: *You are my friends if you do the same.*

Jesus is saying something like this: "I am going to my death to make possible for you a model of creative practice which is not governed by death. From now on this is the only commandment which counts: that you should live your lives as a creative overcoming of death, showing that you are prepared to die because you are not moved by death, and you are doing this to make possible a similar living out for your friends. The measure in which they *are* your friends is the degree in which, thanks to the perception which they have of *your* creative acting out of a life beyond the rule of death, they come to have their imagination expanded in the same way, and they too become capable of entering into this creative living out of a life that is not ruled by death."

That this is exactly the point which Jesus is making, if we don't allow it to be subverted by myths of sacred renunciation, is exactly shown by what follows: he says to his disciples that now they *are* his friends, and not servants, because he has given them to know what he received from the Father, his utterly vivid life, and so on, and it is this which will empower them to go out and give much fruit. The commandment of love, far from being an insistence that we strain our feelings, as it is so often understood, in a sort of grotesque Christian parody, is a commandment to create a visible and *imitable* human history, living a life that is empowered by an imagination not shaded by death in a free and diverse imitation of the human story created and lived out by Jesus.

I'm sorry if this is somewhat complicated, but what I have sought to emphasize is the way in which Jesus' giving of the Holy Spirit is his handing over of a flexible paradigm and an open definition of the discovery of a real meaning and truth by allowing us to live out creatively diverse stories which are found, however, to be all rooted in this one, unique story of self-giving up to death. It is only thus that I manage to find sense in John's language.[6]

Opening Up Creation

There is another dimension to what John understood of Jesus' imagination: something less apparent but no less important. It is not so much something different from what we have described as a different way of describing the same thing. Throughout his Gospel John scatters hints of what he said in the prologue: that God created the world with and by means of Christ. This is especially emphasized in the way John presents Jesus as working on the Sabbath. There is a particular justification for Jesus' work on the Sabbath which is found only in John. Jesus answers those who question this practice:

> My Father carries on working until the present, and I work also.
> (John 5:17)

Now, please note: this is not the sort of obvious answer which "sensible people" would give, because they have a general notion of God, who, of course, works the whole time, so, why shouldn't we carry on working as well? We have something rather more dense. Jesus is formally denying that God is resting on the Sabbath, a solemn contradiction of Genesis. God is creative effervescence, constantly and lovingly creating, so that the institution of the Sabbath, while it may be important for us humans to rest, is a symbol of creation yet to be completed and still needing its fullness. So Jesus also works, that is to

---

6. It seems to me that it is perhaps for this reason that John does not include at this moment an account of the institution of the Eucharist: not because he does not believe in it, for it will have been the normal practice in his community, but because he wanted much more fully to underline the "existential" sense of "Do this in memory of me," so that the Eucharist should not be an empty sign but the culminating celebration of a real way of living.

say, brings creation to its proper fulfillment, making people whole on the Sabbath. These works he does not only for the benefit of those who get cured, but as signs. Such signs are real acts which point to something more than themselves. They point to the real work which Jesus is carrying out through his creative self-giving to death as a model for us to do the same, that is to say, bringing about the possibility of the fulfillment of all history.

Let us look at a further insinuation of this in the story of the man blind from birth in John 9. He was born blind, which is to say that in him creation was quite definitely not completed. On a Sabbath Jesus brings to fulfillment the work of creation, thus giving glory to God. The former blind man even goes so far as to say (and John's literary style and subtlety are, at least for me, a source of immense pleasure):

Never since the world began [ek tou aiōnos] has it been heard that someone opened the eyes of one born blind. (John 9:32)

That is, Jesus is fulfilling what was missing from the beginning of creation. That this is, obviously, a sign for everyone rather than just a gift for the blind man is shown by the discussion which follows between Jesus and some Pharisees who were present at his meeting with the (now) former blind man. Jesus points out that those who know themselves to be blind receive their sight, while those who think that they see participate in the mechanism of expulsion (they have just thrown the former blind man out of the synagogue) and see absolutely nothing.

Jesus insists that the works which he carries out ought to bear witness that he comes from the Father. He tells this to those who pick up stones, preparing to kill him, in John 10:31–39. For us to be able to understand that Jesus' works give witness to the Father, I think that it is vital for us to understand what Jesus is saying to them. He is *not* saying: "Look here, I've done plenty of good works, and that means I'm a holy sort of fellow," but rather "Look, what I am doing could not be done except by the Creator of all things himself. Even if you don't particularly like me, at least look at the creative works and the signs. By whom else could these things be done if not by the Creator? So, He is working through me, and that does indeed authenticate the fact that I am a dependable representative of God."

The fact that people hate him and seek to do away with him, *even though they have seen the works which he carries out,* suggests that these people are not just made uncomfortable by him, but that they are in fact locked into a profound aversion to creation itself. They are clinging on to a form, futile, useless, and shot through with death, of incomplete creation, and resisting being completely created — which means coming to be completely, dependently, and joyfully creative, following what we saw in our discussion of Jesus' "flexible paradigm."

When, in John 16:20–21, Jesus uses the language of a woman in labor to describe his going to his death, John places in his mouth the same metaphor which Paul uses to describe the whole of creation in travail, through the persecutions which bring to light the children of God (Rom. 8:18–23). Jesus' self-giving up to death *is* the fulfillment of creation, the putting of creation into a state of labor, so that we also, by our creative imitation of him in the midst of the order of death can come to be the fully created creatures which God always wanted us to be, and with us, the whole of creation. It is because of this that Jesus' last word before his death in John's Gospel is *tetelestai:* it is accomplished, it has been brought to fulfillment. This means *that creation itself has been brought to fulfillment by his self-giving up to death in order to open up for us a creative way by which we may come to participate fully in creation.* It can be understood, then, why the resurrection happens on the first day of the week, in the garden. Creation has started again, a creation in which the tomb is empty.

I emphasize this point, subtly hinted at by John, because if we are going to come close to recovering the eschatological imagination, I don't think that we can do it while we imagine Jesus dragged boredly to an unnecessary death. John understood Jesus to be possessed by a completely extraordinary imagination, utterly fixed on God, in such a way that *as a human being* he could produce the final touch of divine creation, which consists in creatively imagining a way in which we — the rest of the human race — might be set free from what seems to be our very nature: mortality, and the way in which death runs our lives. John also gives a very important indication of how Jesus himself conceived of what he was doing: he speaks of the joy of Jesus. Jesus draws nigh to his death with joy. His creative work is perhaps — how could it be more — solemn, and in our eyes, terrifying. Perhaps it did produce a trembling and a sweat of blood, but it was conceived in joy by someone whose creative mind was fixed on an inexhaustible creative joy. This joy is something which he wanted his disciples to have:

And now I come to thee, and these things I speak in the world, that they might have my joy fulfilled in themselves. (John 17:13)

He had told them before, that, after they have seen him at the resurrection, they will rejoice, and no one will take away their joy (John 16:22). This joy, like the peace which Jesus gives but the world cannot give, is the joy which flows from the fixing of the mind on the utter vivaciousness of the living, effervescent God who knows not death, a fixing of the mind which will be possible for them after Jesus has opened the possibility for mortal humans (shot through with death) to participate in that creative love and life by going to his death. John is not the only witness to this. We have already read in the epistle to the Hebrews:

... [our] eyes fixed on Jesus the author and finisher of our faith, who *for the joy that was set before him* endured the cross, despising the shame, and is set down at the right hand of the throne of God. (Heb. 12:1–2)

Conclusion

We have looked at how John understood Jesus to have conceived of what he was doing, an understanding that became possible among the apostolic group only after the stripping from the perception of God of any involvement in violence, and in the degree to which it became clear that God had authentically given himself to be known by means of a creative act of love which could be revealed only in the concrete story, lived out and staged, by which Jesus opened up for us the access to God. God's love for Jesus and for us consisted exactly in the sending of Jesus, that is to say, in God's being deliberately and intentionally the source of Jesus' self-giving; and Jesus' love for his Father consisted exactly in his obedience to his Father, an obedience which consists in a faithful imitation, or human *mise-en-scène* of God's immortal vivacity in the midst of human death (cf. John 14:31). I say this because it will allow us to examine another point when we come to examine the eschatological imagination: Jesus' imagination fixed on God's death-less effervescence. God's love cannot be understood, in the first place, somewhat counter to a certain tendency of ours, as a series of passionate heart throbs or the pouring forth of a general sweetness. It consisted, and consists, in making available a rather particular human living out. Perhaps this is not what we want. What we want, when we want to be loved, is to be taken, cuddled, told that everything's okay, that we're okay, that there's a general feeling of all being well. We want to be made to feel better about the situation in which we find ourselves. Well, it was not thus, apparently, that Jesus imagined love.

He seems to have insisted on bringing into being something which doesn't correspond at all to our desires, like a boat which is heading off somewhere else. It is not as though he is consoling us in our small, timorous identities; rather he is furnishing the means for us to take part in a different show, something which calls us to be something different from what we thought we were. In the light of this, in the next chapter we're going to examine Jesus' preaching of the kingdom and the coming into being of the Church.

Chapter 4

The Heavens Opened, and the Kingdom Out of Joint

In our last chapter we saw something of how John understood Jesus' creative imagination as he went to his death in order to create the possibility that we might follow him in forging stories of a rich diversity which would be the fulfillment of creation. That is to say, we saw how Jesus inaugurated a diverse visible practice which was to become the constant and free re-creation of his story by us. Another way to describe what Jesus was doing is to say that he was bringing in the kingdom, and yet a third way is to say that he was founding the Church.

I wanted to lay stress on a somewhat delicate matter, difficult to describe exactly, which seems to me to be of extreme importance, and that is how strange Jesus' project is, how odd, how out of synch. This we saw in the case of John, who is perhaps the theologian who most fully worked out what still remains unsynthesized in the other texts of the apostolic witness, as we looked at his teaching on the strangeness of God and thus the strangeness of God's love. That is, Jesus' Father is not known by everyone and is not known easily. The reason is not that the Father is weird, but that our understanding, our education, and our imagination are marked by death and its consequences. And this means that the Father's love is not so easy to understand because it is not necessarily what we want, and this not because it is weird, but because our wanting, our desire, is also marked by death. In this way it is quite possible that the coming into existence of the Father's loving project — the fulfillment of creation — may pass us by unless we learn to seek it out and to find it with a gaze somewhat different from the normal.

Let us try to move up close to this feeling of weirdness, that is, let's try to understand something of the rules of the game by which we too may come to participate in the bringing about of the new heaven and the new earth, something of the rules of grammar necessary for us to be able to write with our lives stories that are the *other* story, not the tired story of the violence of the world. Jesus did not confine himself just to organizing a death in order to take away its sting for us; he also left us elements to enrich our creation of a diverse story. These elements reveal at the same time the sort of project that he thought that he was bringing about and something of what he considered to be our difficulties in entering into the game.

Heaven Open

We're going to look at three rather different stories to see where they take us. At the beginning of John's Gospel, when Jesus is recruiting the ones he wants to be his witnesses to accompany him in his work, so that they may afterward take the good news to others, he calls a certain Nathanael. This Nathanael was a good Israelite, a little grumpy, half incredulous, to judge by his few words like "Can any good thing come out of Nazareth?" (John 1:46). However, he goes with Philip to meet Jesus, who tells him that he is an authentic Israelite, that is, son of Israel, without duplicity. Nathanael asks him why he says this, and Jesus replies that he saw him sitting beneath the fig tree before Philip called him, at which Nathanael rushes to acknowledge Jesus' messianic titles — that he is the king of Israel. Jesus is surprised to be so easily recognized and tells him that he will see greater things yet, and then adds:

> Verily, verily I say unto you, Hereafter ye shall see heaven open and the angels of God ascending and descending upon the son of man. (John 1:51)

You will remember what incident this phrase refers to: Jacob, the first and authentic Israel, falls into a sleep, in which he sees a ladder and the angels of God ascending and descending (Gen. 28:12). To this authentic son of Israel there is promised the same experience, but with the difference that there is no ladder swung between heaven and earth, or rather the Son of man, that is, Jesus, is himself Jacob's ladder.

Here at the very beginning of his public ministry, Jesus explains to a group of witnesses what will be the centerpoint of their experience in the terms we have seen: by accompanying him they will learn to see heaven open and angels ascending and descending on Jesus. His whole project for them is explained in this line, everything we have been looking at. The opening of heaven will be the making accessible of the Father who knows not death and the presence of Jesus as risen victim, by means of whom heaven stands open and there begins that flux of heavenly riches and abundance for those who perceive him as the access to the Father.

At another quite different moment of the apostolic witness, in the Acts of the Apostles, after the Ascension, Stephen has to defend himself before the Sanhedrin. His defense consists in an attempt to tell the story of Israel anew, a revisionist rewriting, an attempt which does not commend him to the upholders of the tradition, the bulwarks of the official story. What Stephen does is to tell the story which everybody already knew, from rather an odd angle, from the angle which came to light after the Holy Spirit made it possible to tell the story of the lynch from the viewpoint of the victim. The conclusion to the story is obvious, and well known by all. What is interesting is the last line of the story, just before the lynching begins:

> But Stephen, being full of the Holy Spirit, fixed his gaze on heaven and saw the glory of God and Jesus standing at the right hand of God, and said: Behold I see the heavens opened, and the Son of man standing at the right hand of God.
>
> (Acts 7:55–56)

His hearers react as can be expected: they have just heard an open blasphemy, that is, a new definition of God which includes the dead man, and *stopping their ears and crying out with a loud voice* so as not to have to hear the blasphemy, they rush upon Stephen and kill him.

Luke apparently writes like a Hollywood scriptwriter, and if his account were to be taken to the screen, we could imagine the moment at which Stephen fixes his gaze on heaven. He is standing in the midst of a raging Sanhedrin, bathed in a strange light, sweet celestial chords can be heard, and then comes the martyrdom. Well, thrilling though it be, I don't think that it's really about that. It makes more sense to understand that what Stephen was doing was what Jesus had promised Nathanael that he would be able to do: see heaven open and the rest. This was precisely what began to happen from the Ascension. It was not just that the last seconds of Stephen's life were bathed in this heavenly light, but that what enabled him to tell the story he told to the high priest and his colleagues was exactly the fact that he was already living this vision; he was able to tell the new story which the risen victim had made possible, and, furthermore, live out this story in an absolutely coherent way, as if death did not exist, and do it to the end. He even managed to finish off his own opera-plot in a faithful imitation of that of Jesus (which is also a diverse creation), by praying that his death not be held against his executioners. That is, he ends his own creation with the last act of disassociating himself from the violent story of this world, which is to leave it behind, with no resentment, no desire for revenge.

Here we have what the Church has rightly called the protomartyr: the first witness; and that to which he witnesses is the vivaciousness of God revealed by the dead and risen victim and the power this victim gives to create heaven.

The end of the apostolic witness, one of the strangest books ever to have been written, and which I hope we will be able to read with different eyes after these pages, is a long meditation on the open heaven, in the center of which are the throne of God and the slaughtered lamb, the only one who can open the book and the seals which are the key to the true story of everything. That is to say, this book is, all of it, centered on the same vision promised to Nathanael and lived by Stephen. I want to direct your attention to something close to the end, where the seer says this:

> And I saw a new heaven and a new earth: for the first heaven and the first earth were passed away; and there was no more sea. And I John saw the holy city, new Jerusalem, coming down from God out of heaven, prepared as a bride adorned for her husband.... And I saw no Temple therein: for the Lord God almighty and the Lamb are the Temple of it. And the city had no need of the sun, neither of the moon, to shine in it: for the glory of God did lighten it, and the Lamb is the light thereof.
> (Rev. 21:1–2, 22–23)

I hope that it is obvious to you that we are talking, allowing for the appropriate literary differences, about exactly the same vision of which Jesus had spoken to Nathanael and which Stephen saw. But there has been a development, and an important one, not only in the sense of filling out the vision with all sorts of glories. The angels have been suppressed (on the other hand there's no shortage of them in the book of Revelation), and instead of them it is the new Jerusalem which is coming down. Its epicenter is not a temple (unlike the earthly Jerusalem, which had been destroyed by the time our text was written), but God himself is its epicenter and its light, shining out by means of the lamb who is, of course, slaughtered. That is to say, the risen Jesus is the mediator of God's light, the one by means of whom heaven is open. However we are not dealing with an individual vision to console someone on the point of martyrdom, but it is a whole city that is coming down from heaven. That is to say, the Church *is* the collective living out of the opening of heaven, as something which is coming down from God, made possible by the risen victim.

Look at the progression in our three stories of the open heaven: first we saw the witness chosen to see heaven open, one of Jesus' companions chosen to be able to bear witness to everything lived and worked by him; then we saw the "ordinary Christian," that is, someone who was not an apostolic witness, who learns to create his own diverse story in the light of the risen victim; and finally we understand that the whole project which Jesus initiated *is* the coming down of a new, collective, story, woven out of the many stories of those who have allowed themselves to be illuminated by the God who gives himself to be mediated by the slaughtered lamb, that is, the stories of those who, in the superlative language of the seer, have washed white their garments in the blood of the lamb.

The Apostle, the ordinary Christian, the Church, all centered on the heaven opened by the risen victim seated at the right hand of God. What does this tell us about what Jesus was doing and how he understood it?

The Preaching of the Kingdom

At the beginning of the Gospels of Matthew and Mark, Jesus sets out to preach, and what he says is, apparently, simple:

> The time has reached its fullness and the kingdom of God is at hand; change your hearts and believe the good news.
>
> (Mark 1:15)

First he announces the closeness of the kingdom of God and works signs. At the same time he begins to choose people to be his witnesses. And he chooses twelve. This already tells us something about what he thought he was doing, that is, he was symbolically refounding Israel, with its twelve tribes. It's very important that we notice this, since this number continues to be stressed until Pentecost. The ones who were chosen themselves understood that they had been chosen to bring about a restoration of the kingdom of Israel: that's why they ask Jesus just before the Ascension if it is now that he will restore the kingdom of Israel (Acts 1:6). And immediately after the Ascension and before Pentecost, they choose Matthias to fill the empty place among the twelve which had been left by Judas. Their criterion for choosing was that the one chosen should have accompanied Jesus and the twelve original witnesses during the whole of Jesus' public ministry up until his Ascension. That is, it was understood that fundamental to what Jesus wanted to do was the bringing about of some sort of new symbolic Israel, and that what makes this possible is the presence of people who had lived through the whole process of the change of mind and of heart produced by the ministry and passion of Jesus and then his presence as risen victim.

Let us be clear, then, that whatever it was that Jesus thought that he was doing, he didn't want to leave everything in the dark, but he used the language, the expectations, and the symbolism which people already had to point up the sort of thing that he wanted to bring about. Now, please notice this: he is leaving something like a reader's guide, some rules of grammar by which to read what he was doing, and these rules of grammar point toward what I have called a "subversion from within." Jesus was not saying: "The kingdom of heaven is so ineffable and mysterious that there is no language to describe it, so I leave you with a vague movement of search in this life whose sense will be known only in the next." Neither is he saying: "The kingdom of God is the fulfillment of the Israel which you all know and love, with all its hopes and expectations." Well, of course you recognize these two tendencies: they are the same ones we saw when we were looking at the principle of analogy in the first chapter, and we will return to them at the end of this one.

Jesus is setting up something strange, and he uses the language of Israel and its traditions; because of this there is something of a correspondence between this human story (which was already a story of the human overcoming of violent human stories), and the heavenly story which he is bringing into being; however, what Jesus is setting up is not too closely identified with that story. The apostles' question which we have seen in Acts shows that their tendency, like the good proto-Catholics they were, was to imagine too close an identification between the story of Israel and that of the new Israel, between what they represented and heaven. That is to say: they hadn't yet grasped the element of weirdness and knocking off-guard which there is in the bringing into existence of what would later be called the Church.

Now, that was not the case with Jesus. He was indeed teaching about the arrival of something which is, for his listeners, very weird. That's why he has to teach in parables. And please note the justification which he gives for teaching in parables. He quotes Isaiah when he says:

> Listen as you will and you will not understand; look as you will and you will not see, because this people's heart has waxed gross. They are dull of hearing and have closed their eyes against seeing and their ears against hearing lest they be turned to me that I may heal them. (Matt. 13:14–15 quoting Isa. 6:9–10; cf. Mark 4:12 and Luke 8:9–10)

That is, there is no direct understanding of the kingdom: it is a strange thing, and people's minds are dulled, which is exactly what we would expect as a result of what we've seen about the human condition, our own included, shot through with death.

It's worth our while to stop a little to see what this teaching in parables consists in. The parables are highly creative little stories sprung from Jesus' imagination and have as their aim helping people to overcome their being blocked up with respect to God and his project. However, behold, they are two-edged weapons, capable of different interpretations. It is perfectly possible to interpret the greater part in terms of a violent God. In that case the parables only serve to reinforce what people already think anyway, and they move on no further. What I'm suggesting is that this would be the "dull-hearted" reading of the parables. At the same time it is perfectly possible to read the same parables as obliging us to overcome this vision. This means that there is an interpretation for those who understand and that what they understand will increase exponentially, and there is another interpretation for those who do not understand, so that what little they do understand is in the process of being lost, for they will get into an ever more tied-up and painful understanding of the things of God.[1] And here it is not worth our ef-

---

1. Here I would like to point out that this is exactly what Girard understands in his exposition of mimetic desire: whoever has not grasped the mimetic workings of desire, and because of this begun to come out of being enmeshed in mimetic rivalry, will twist everything up in an ever greater frustration; whoever has begun to move in a pacific mimesis will understand very well the messes which he or she is leaving behind and will understand all things creatively and pacifically. See, for example, Girard's discussion

fort to stop and worry about a possible elitism on the part of Jesus: in fact, there is just that elitism. Time after time Jesus points out things like: many are called and few are chosen; or: to the one who has much, will much be given, but the one who has little, even what he has will be taken away. Jesus is no populist preacher!

Let me take a parable to show you what I'm trying to say, Matthew 13:47–50:

> Again, the kingdom of heaven is like unto a net, that was cast into the sea, and gathered of every kind: which, when it was full, they drew to shore, and sat down, and gathered the good into vessels, but cast the bad away. So shall it be at the end of the world: the angels shall come forth, and sever the wicked from among the just, and shall cast them into the furnace of fire: there shall be wailing and gnashing of teeth.

Now, there's a perfectly admissible reading of this which you all know: that in the Church there are all manners of people, good and bad alike, and that all eventually reach the shore of death, where a great divine separation awaits them, with a subsequent punishment for those who deserve it. But is it really the case that Jesus wanted to say something so obvious to people who didn't need anybody to frighten them with more stories from beyond the grave? Is it the case that *in any parable at all* Jesus is seeking to hand out insider-information about the "afterward"? Personally, I rather doubt it. It seems to me that his technique is much more interesting. I suggest that he is taking for granted a certain understanding of God and seeking to introduce a hidden shock into it. He knows very well that, were he to speak directly about God, people would answer him back quoting contrary proof-texts, and they could go round and round in circles indefinitely. Because of this he is prepared to work in hostile territory, using the imaginative world of his hearers, but putting into it a little time-bomb which, when it explodes, can cause a change in that imaginative world.

In the case of the parable which I quoted for you, how would it be if *instead of information about the end* it were rather a teaching about how to live in the here and now, in the time before the end. In that case, the function of the story is a little different. Instead

---

of the double message in the works of Shakespeare in *A Theater of Envy* — *William Shakespeare* (New York: Oxford University Press, 1991).

of furnishing us with details of a judgment after death, it is rather an insistence on *not exercising any type of judgment before death.* When he says: "There will be wailing and gnashing of teeth" let us not take it as a threat, but as: "Leave it for *another* to cause wailing and gnashing of teeth. Let it be *there* and not *here.* Do not you exercise any sort of judgment or separation between good and evil people *now.* In this way you will be building the kingdom of heaven." It wouldn't be a bad exercise to attempt a re-reading of other parables following this formula, and before the end of this book we will be doing something similar with the parable of the sheep and the goats. For now let this slight example suffice. But please note once again in what Jesus' technique consists: it consists in introducing a little subversion from within into the normal imagination in order to open out our horizons a little with respect to who God is and what are his ways.

Let us take another kind of parable: Jesus says to his hearers that the kingdom of heaven is like leaven which a woman put into three measures of meal, till the whole is leavened (Matt. 13:33). Here the use of "leaven" is interesting, since on other occasions Jesus tells his disciples to beware of the leaven of the Pharisees and the Sadducees (Matt. 16:6). I suggest to you that Jesus is saying that what he is bringing into existence, that is, the good news about God which will be shown by the inauguration of the innocent victim, will serve as a leaven which little by little will effect a change in the whole of human society in such a way that all human living together will be shot through, fermented, by this possibility. The leaven of the Pharisees and the Sadducees would be the way of building a human society starting from an apparent goodness which rather serves to mask an expulsive violence and ferments nothing at all, but is the pious grinding on of business as usual.

The grain of mustard would be something similar: Jesus is saying that the little sign which he will bring about by going to his death, of little promise as it may appear, will produce a great result *in terms of social structure,* so that the birds which would normally have dedicated themselves to eating up any available seed can nest in its branches. What Jesus is bringing to existence is something which will even be capable of offering hospitality to those who would have been its principal enemies: and all this has happened! It is a fact that we live in a society which prides itself on making space for its own persecutors and offers a whole series of advantages to people who want nothing to do with the Christian religion, and even persecute it, but who, in order to do so, lay hold of all the advantages which have been produced by a way of living together founded on the possibility of the innocence of the victim.

Please notice that this has nothing to do with moralism, but is a very realistic explanation of the kind of social change which was to be produced in a society where, however invisibly, the interpretation which Jesus brought to existence, that of the innocence of the victim, is seeping through. That is to say, Jesus is explaining very long term what it is that he was doing, in a way which is only just comprehensible today, and how much less would it have been before his death and resurrection! But let us continue with our exploration of the weirdness of the kingdom.

Shaking Up the Agents...

The weirdness of the kingdom is not only pointed up by means of parables, whose more long-term function we will be studying in another chapter, but also by the way in which Jesus deals with those who follow him. Apart from those whom he chose to found, by means of their testimony, the new story of the subversion from within of Israel, that is, the twelve, there are a series of accounts which indicate that the kingdom produces a shaking-up, knocks people out of joint. We can see this in the accounts of those who wanted to follow Jesus. A scribe says to him that he will follow him "whithersoever thou goest" (Matt. 8:19), and Jesus answers him that the Son of man has nowhere to lay his head. Here I don't think it's an attempt to test the scribe by saying to him: "Well, okay, if you follow me there will be many occasions on which you will not even have a place to spend the night." I think that the use of "Son of man," the figure from Daniel 7:13 — which consists, by the way, in a vision of the open heaven and a man on the clouds beside the Ancient — suggests that Jesus is saying something a little different: "Look, in this business of following me, don't think that I'm taking you to some safe place, or anything like that. The one who follows the Son of man *does not have a place,* for in every place he or she will have to create the story which comes from the open heaven, and that story means that that place *will not be their place,* for the story which comes from the open heaven *is* the story of the one who has no place, the one who does not find himself at home in the midst of the world of human violence."

Then a disciple says to Jesus:

Lord, let me first go and bury my father. But Jesus said to him
"Follow me and let the dead bury the dead." (Matt. 8:22)

Let's try to imagine how thrown that disciple would have been
with this answer, and indeed, what a shocking answer it is, against
all piety. It is evident that Jesus is not referring to really dead people,
for these can bury no one, busy as they are about their own decom-
position. Rather he is saying: this piety of burying the dead is proper
to a culture based on death and has nothing to do with the piety of
those who are building the kingdom which knows not death. Get out
of the culture of death, leave it behind, and build with me the culture
which is coming into existence.

We could multiply passages like these. The kingdom knocks out of
joint because it is apparently so little religious: Jesus' disciples appear scandalously normal, not fasting (Matt. 9:14), unworried by
ritual purity (Mark 7:1–5). Jesus seems to insist that, unless there be
a break with the normal system of kinship, there can be no following
of him in the construction of the kingdom: he puts the institution of
marriage into question, suggesting that it is better to have nothing to
do with it, for those who can accept this. We've already seen that he
considers human reproduction unnecessary as a way of overcoming
death, because God can create infinite humans without need of it —
even human reproduction itself is shaded by death.

Then we have those passages where Jesus recognizes that what he
has come to bring will not produce peace and social harmony, but
rather the reverse: it will divide families. He knew very well that
from the moment when the paradigm of the innocent victim is installed, which is what he comes to do, the normal human mechanism
for creating peace is over, that is, the all-against-one of sacralized vic-
timization, apparently blessed by god, has broken down. And those
who live this out will be considered impious and traitors; and they
will be, because that person will be betraying the order of this world.
Because of this, the person who perceives someone as unjustly persecuted, the one who gives a cup of water to someone held by others to
be a traitor, a vile threat, an element of contamination, that person
will have a prophet's reward, because they will in fact have acted as
a prophet by perceiving that the one considered evil is hated without
a cause.

I think that with this we are recovering something of the weirdness of the kingdom which is coming and understanding why it has
to be weird: the strangeness is that of the project of installing life

in a culture of death which works according to its own rules. I suggest that no story of our participation in this project can pass this weirdness by: it is one of the rules of grammar for the forging of our story according to the flexible paradigm of Jesus. We will see that this strangeness, this being knocked out of joint, operates not only on a social level, but touches our most intimate being.

Inappropriate Vocations

In this world there are many very fine, stable people, noble and serene. There are people pleasant to the eye, respectable, people who would be natural leaders. We all know this: if you want to sell something, or you want your party to win an election, it is of first importance that you find someone attractive, as if to say: look what sort of people are on our side, the very best, the prettiest, the most outstanding athletes, the people of highest social quality, greatest intellectual weight, and so on. We have seen that Jesus indeed had a project which depended on provoking an imitation, on making itself attractive so that all manner of people might begin to reproduce that living out. Let us imagine a group of disciples formed by people like that rich young man who came up to Jesus. It would be devastating, something like having a congregation of priests formed by the handsome hunks who can be found on a weekend in one of our shopping malls, or of an evening working out in a health club, or a congregation of nuns chosen among the winners of beauty contests, or Christian Dior models in Paris. Who would not want to be part of such a movement?

Well, no. Jesus does not choose people like this, and neither does he lower his criteria for those of this type who are interested in him, much though he may appreciate them. If they want to follow him, they have to leave behind the order of which they form such a solid part. Furthermore, Jesus doesn't even know how to choose people well. Let us stop a little to look at his candidate for leader of his group of witnesses, the fisherman Simon whom he calls "rock." It is difficult to imagine someone less evidently "rock." To judge by the accounts which Peter and his companions have passed on to us, he was the impetuous sort, but of little consistency. That is, he promised a great deal and was unable to live up to it, as when he told Jesus that he would follow him, come what may, and shortly afterward he abandoned him. He throws himself overboard to walk on the sea, in imitation of Jesus, and seconds later is up to his neck. He is, besides, the bubbly sort who says a lot of things on the spur of the moment, without them meaning much. This we see in his behavior during the transfiguration (see Mark 9:5–6 and parallels). I imagine that when, in answer to Jesus' question

Who do *you* say that I am? (Mark 8:29)

Peter declares him to be the Messiah, the Son of God, this was not a solemn declaration, after consultation with the other disciples, but another of his wild shots,[2] and that then Jesus, somewhat surprised, I suspect, by his having hit the bull's-eye, had to give to this flash in the pan all the weight which it deserved: recognizing that the most solid divine revelation had arrived by means of a conspicuously un-solid vehicle. In fact, here we see Jesus' technique: he often takes a person in her wild shot, and gives to it a special importance, far beyond what the person in question could imagine, speaking to that person as if she were very different from what in fact she is. This is what I call an inappropriate vocation.

I understand it like this: our identity is formed by the desires and currents of this world, just as we saw in the first chapter, and it is nor-mally a fragile identity, tangled up and full of contradictions, as are the desires by which we are shot through and which have formed our consciousness. In fact the conscious "I" of each one of us has very little idea of who we are, very little capacity to understand what we are, in point of truth, doing, what hidden dramas of self-punishment, of vengeance, and so on, we are creating. That is, our level of self-deception is pretty high. Jesus understands very well that to this "me," God does not even speak, because it is a mask "me" which only has the ears and eyes of this world. Because of this Jesus doesn't speak to this "me" either, but calls into being another "me," rather as a hypnotist does, a "me" which apparently has nothing to do with who we are, and may be its complete reverse, but which is a calling into becoming something we do not even suspect, entering into the process of the creation of a different story. Jesus tells Peter, the im-petuous one, that as a young man he did exactly what he liked, and that as an old man he will be borne to where he would rather not go. The sandiest of Jesus' followers, the one most like the son who said "yes" but did not, rather than the son who said "no" but did, God made into a rock by means of his martyrdom.

---

2. "ex sese et non ex consensu ecclesiae"(!).

It is this, I think, which is behind what Jesus says in Luke 10:20, when the seventy-two return from their mission:

> Rejoice not that the spirits are subject to you, but rather because your names are written in heaven.

It is not the acts which they carry out which count, but rather that those acts are signs that there is a new identity being created in the lives of each one of them and that that is what is most important: the new "I" which God is calling into existence. For "names written in heaven" read: new identities which God is bringing into existence in the degree to which we begin to participate in the creation of the new and death-less story, the story that is heaven. In the first epistle of St. John we read something similar:

> My friends, we are already children of God, even though it has not yet appeared what we will be; but we know that when Jesus appears and we see him as he is, we will be like him. All who have placed this hope in Jesus are purifying themselves to be pure as Jesus is pure. (1 John 3:2–3)

This seems to mean something like this: our true identity is still to come, and we will know it only when the story which Jesus inaugurated is unveiled in all its fullness, when we will see what has been our real participation, our real creation in flexible imitation of his own.

Once more it is seen that the coming into existence of the kingdom incorporates a whole lot of people of no importance, of no apparent worth, and even these people are knocked out of joint, called in highly inappropriate ways, to come to be something which they are not, something which is a being stretched out of themselves beyond their limits, or, as St. Paul says, referring to this same question, in one of the most notable passages of Scripture:

> But God hath chosen the foolish things of the world to confound the wise; and God hath chosen the weak things of the world to confound the things which are mighty; and base things of the world, and things which are despised, hath God chosen, yea and *things which are not, to bring to nought the things that are.* (1 Cor. 1:27–28)

These lines give us the whole meaning: by means of Jesus, the Creator of all things is bringing creation to existence out of nothing. This preferring of the weak and the foolish has nothing to do with any resentment or desire to turn everything upside down, as at times we imagine with a mentality which still conceives of God as brandishing some sort of vengeance against those who have it well in life. It is rather the case that only that which is fragile, weak, precarious according to the order of this world is capable of allowing itself to be broken so as to be created anew. The rest, that which is strong, wise, and so on, has its identity so anchored in its formation by the desires of this world that it is not capable of that breaking open of identity so that the new "I" may be called to existence. Sadly, that's how it is. The vocations to the kingdom are inappropriate because only that which is vulnerable can allow itself to be broken in order to be built up again. When Jesus tells Nicodemus that no one can see the kingdom of heaven unless they be born from above, or anew (John 3:3), he is speaking precisely about this unsuspected "I" whose identity is forged out of sight of who we think we are by people whose imagination is fixed on the things that are above, and whose creation of a story sets out from there.

How to Create This Other Story

Perhaps now we can look at the bit of Jesus' proclamation which, coming first, I have left till last. Remember that his preaching was:

> The time has reached its fullness and the kingdom of God is at hand; change your hearts and believe the good news.
> (Mark 1:15)

I have spoken first about the "believe in the good news" part so that we can draw close to the "change your hearts" with a different gaze. There is a way of understanding this message, helped by a certain translation of the Greek *metanoiéte* — probably itself translating the Hebrew *shuv* — which falls straight into a moralistic interpretation and so nullifies its meaning. According to this vision, Jesus went out preaching so that we should get ourselves in good moral order to be able to participate in a kingdom which is only for those who have got themselves in order. By this stage of our study it is possible to glimpse another interpretation of the same thing: our being able to change heart is made possible by our believing in the good news. In the degree to which we learn to fix our mind on God's absolute vivaciousness and effervescence, goodness and lovingkindness, without ambiguity or violence, we can learn to leave behind the person we thought that we were, participating actively in the bringing to being of a new person, not formed by the desires of this world.

This means something rather important: that there is no story at all of our participation in creation, according to the flexible paradigm of the heavenly story, which is not what is usually called a story of conversion. By a story of conversion I don't mean one of those accounts of how I was bound by this or that vice, had an overpowering experience, and have now managed to leave it all behind me — though such changes are by no means to be belittled when they happen. However, they are incidents, and not stories. Someone can give up doing something held a vice only to turn into a persecutor of those who lack his same moral fiber. That is not a Christian conversion. Authentic converts always write a story of their discovery of mercy, which means that they learn to create mercy, and not despite, for others. This rule of grammar we find set out in the parable of the servant who was let off all he owed by the king, his creditor, but who didn't forgive the tiny debt his colleague had with him (Matt. 18:23–34).

To see this more clearly, let us consider the following: the whole apostolic witness is structured, so to speak, around two stories of conversion. Most notoriously the story of the conversion of Saul into Paul, of the persecutor into the messenger of grace. This story is known to all, and often does us poor service, since, following its Lucan version, it tends to privilege a somewhat dramatic notion of conversion, like a thunderclap from a clear sky, immediately producing a new person. There is no shortage of elements which tend to modify this fixing upon the immediate, such as the fact that Paul went off, after his experience, to a part of Syria which was known as Arabia in those days, where he stayed for three years before going up to Jerusalem. But it is the immediate version which gets the attention. The other conversion story which underlies many of the texts of the apostolic witness, and which is perhaps more important, as it is more subtle, is the story of the conversion of Peter. There are a series of very early witnesses which suggest that the Gospel which we know as Mark's was written in special proximity to Peter, taking up and working through many of his memories, and this would explain the fact that Peter doesn't come out especially well in that account: his preaching of the Gospel could not but be the story of someone who had betrayed his best friend and who had had to revise his whole life in the light of this best friend appearing first to him, without any element of recrimination or blaming.

John suggests the same, and does so in an especially beautiful way. Let's pause beside Peter's conversion in John. Remember that Peter gets as far as the courtyard of the high priest's house, and there he warms himself with others before a charcoal fire (John 18:18). It is there, beside the fire, that he denies three times that he knows Jesus. Then in John 21, Peter jumps into the sea when he hears that the Lord is on the shore to get to him.

> As soon as they were come to land, they saw a fire of coals there, and fish laid thereon and bread. (John 21:9)

The object on which the fish was cooking was, in Greek, exactly the same thing as that before which Peter had denied Jesus: *anthrakian* — a charcoal fire. Imagine Peter's psychology: summoned to recognize Jesus at the same object before which he had betrayed him. Jesus says nothing, but calls them to eat. After they have eaten he unties Peter from the memory of his betrayal by asking him three times if he loves him and then confirms him in his new identity of the one who will feed his sheep.

Something similar is to be found in Luke, when Jesus, predicting Peter's denial, says:

> Simon, Simon, Satan has desired to have you, that he may sift you as wheat: but I have prayed for you that your faith may not fail, and you, when you turn again, strengthen your brethren.
> (Luke 22:31–32)

That is to say, the story of how Simon came to be Peter, the rock, the principal witness to the good news, is the story of someone whose personality had to disintegrate completely, in a process which I imagine to have been extremely painful, so that he might forge and create the story of someone who apparently was not he.

So the two pillars of the apostolic witness, the traitor and the persecutor, offer us something of the rules of grammar by which we come to be that which we are not: there is no beginning to create this new story, this new identity, except starting from how I was brought to the end of myself, sifted like wheat, and had my heart, formed by the deceits and violences of this world, broken open. There is no story empowered by the eschatological imagination that is not a story

of this sort: of how I left Egypt. And this is not owing to some punishing, finger-pointing god, a sort of celestial headmistress, but rather
the weight of glory is too great to be carried in earthen vessels. There
is no story of how "I" was turned into a vessel capable of bearing
glory that is not also the story of the coming to an end of the previous
vessel (cf. 2 Cor. 4:7, 17).

I hope that thus we have gone some way toward "de-moralizing"
the discourse about conversion which surrounds us and which has an
extraordinary tendency to get fixated on the symptoms of weakness
and miss out on the re-creation of the whole "I" by our becoming
empowered to create a different story, which is, after all, what it's
all about.

Raining Down from on High

In the epistle to the Ephesians we read that:

> Each one of us has received the gift in the measure in which
> Christ gave it to us. For this reason Scripture says:
>
> > He rose on high taking with him captives, he gave gifts
> > to men.
>
> And he gave some to be apostles, and others, prophets....
> (Eph. 4:7–8, 11 quoting Ps. 67:19)

The author of this letter is saying that it is when Christ ascends
to heaven, taking death as captive and sitting at the right hand of
God — the vision of the open heaven which we have seen recurring in the apostolic witness — that he rains his gifts down on men,
and these gifts are precisely gifts which empower people to make
of their lives stories sharing in the story which Jesus inaugurated.
That is to say, here we have the same thing as was described by
the seer of Revelation: the Church as something which comes down
out of heaven, a generosity which summons people into being what
they are not, which brings into being people who are not, in order
to create the rich diversity of stories which have their base in, and
complement, the story which Jesus inaugurated by "going" to his
Father.

In this way I have sought to show how the bringing in of the
kingdom and the foundation of the Church are the same thing, and

that both are understood starting from the Ascension. Let us stop a little to get our bearings, since it is quite possible that this way of putting things is so little familiar to you that you are tempted to say to me: "Well, but what has that got to do with our experience of the Church?"

Those of you who have studied eschatology, or ecclesiology, before, will have heard the comment, half ironic and half loyal, of Alfred Loisy, a nineteenth-century French Catholic: Jesus preached the kingdom of God, and what came was the Church. This little quip goes straight to the heart of a whole series of arguments within the Church and between churches, about the relationship between the Church and the kingdom, between a conception of the Church as invisible and a conception of the Church as a highly visible institution. I think that this argument about the relationship between the kingdom and the Church, and hence about the latter's visibility or otherwise, is exactly the same as the one we have already glimpsed when we looked at what I called the principle of analogy. You may remember that in the first chapter we saw two temptations: either the heavenly story, inaugurated by Jesus' death and resurrection, is totally incommensurable with our violent and death-ridden story, to such an extent that we simply have to suspend the attempt to tell a human story and instead wait patiently for the definitive breaking-in of the divine story; or, on the other hand, the heavenly story is not that different from the human story, and the latter can quite easily be a faithful reflection of the former.

Well, the first temptation obliges us, as a logical consequence of the impossibility of telling a redeemed story, to hold that the Church be purely invisible, as the Reformation has insisted. The second holds out, as a consequence of making it too easy to tell the redeemed human story, too familiar a confidence that the visibility of the Church and its institutions are a faithful reflection of the heavenly story. Please notice that in both cases I talk in terms of "telling stories." This is really what it is all about: we are the animals which tell stories, and when we speak of "the Church" we are not talking about anything other than the possibility of telling stories.

What we have seen allows us to take a little distance with relation to what we understand by the Church, not in order to be scandalized by the reality which we perceive, but rather the better to understand what sort of beast we're talking about, so as better to inscribe ourselves in whatever there is of the divine about it. What I'm suggesting is that we all have to do something of the same work as the apostolic group, that is, learn how to subvert from within the reality in which we live so as to learn how to perceive not that which seems too established on earth, with its bludgeoning discourse, its being so bound in with the story of death, but rather that which is coming down from heaven. That is to say, so that the Church comes to be for us a sign of the kingdom. And this doesn't depend on other people than ourselves stopping acting in such an idiotic way, since either they won't stop acting like this, or maybe they aren't acting so idiotically, but we don't know how to perceive what they are doing with eyes formed by the eschatological imagination.

It is worth noting that what is called "ecclesiology," or the discourse about the Church, is a fairly modern discourse, invented in the wake of the Reformation, principally by the Jesuits, and it came into existence in somewhat unfortunate circumstances, for it was born in the midst of a controversy, and on account of this still bears the scars of its defensive and apologetic birth. That is to say it was born to defend the truth of the Church against the devastating critique of the Reformation and for that reason had to have recourse to a series of proofs about Jesus founding the Church in its institutional form, ordaining priests, and so on, matters which no doubt have a nucleus of truth (and there's no way I want to contradict Trent), but in order to be maintained were decked out in a whole way of conceiving of the Church which we're only now learning to get beyond. *Before* the Reformation period there was not "ecclesiology," but rather the treatise of the sacraments, that is, of the signs which in fact constitute ecclesial life.

Maybe, and we have not the space to develop this intuition, we can begin to discover a way of re-creating the Church. It seems to me that, in point of fact, the Church is not that headache which one might suppose reading a certain neo-Catholic (or over-Catholic) press, but an open story, made out of many stories, which flow together around signs of another reality which is coming down out of heaven for us by means of our imaginations being fixed on the things that are above; little stories of the subversion from within of the story of death. This latter story, in our world, as in Jesus' world, gets itself all dressed up in the finery of that which is good, pure, normal, religious, but which leads nowhere, and isn't a sign of anything at all, least of all the arrival in our midst of our own participation in the new creation. How would it be if our Sunday liturgy furnished us with elements for the re-formation of our imaginations, teaching us to fix our minds on the heavenly victim who is giving himself over for us and by means of his words offering us the wherewithal to re-build our little tales?

In the next chapter we will look at two further elements to be incorporated into our creation of the heavenly story: the way in which the eschatological imagination brings about universality and subverts time. This will leave us better placed to study a little eschatology.

Universality and Time

In our last chapter I sought to highlight some of the elements of weirdness which come to light the moment that the eschatological imagination begins to be formed by the fixing of the eyes on the open heaven. I wanted to focus on those elements as rules of grammar for the creative writing of our story in the degree to which we come to have our mind fixed on the things that are above. Now we are going to look at two further dimensions of the eschatological imagination, which will also be two elements more to help us with the forging of our story. We will examine the birth of universality and, although it is somewhat more complicated and experimental, the change which the eschatological imagination introduced into the conception of time.

God Has Showed Me...

When someone asks him if they are few who are saved, Jesus gives a non-reply:

> Strive to enter in by the narrow gate. (Luke 13:24)

That is, quite in line with what we have been seeing, he offers no direct information about the "beyond," of the sort which might satisfy people's curiosity, but rather what he proposes is a lived attitude in the here and now which flows into the "beyond." However, as part of his attempt to shake up his compatriots' presumption of a high degree of continuity between what they live and salvation, he takes advantage of the question to suggest that what Abraham, Isaac, Jacob, and all the prophets will live in the kingdom of God doesn't necessarily square with the image which his listeners have of them, for many of his listeners have nothing in common with these their forebears. Then he suggests something rather important:

And also from east and west, from north and south will they come to recline at banquet in the Kingdom of God. (Luke 13:29)

This may seem very obvious to us, accustomed as we are to Christian life among gentility, where Jews who believe in Jesus are a tiny minority. But it was not always thus! We must make some imaginative effort to understand how odd this would have seemed. Certainly the Jews knew that there were good foreigners, for example, the centurion in the same Gospel of Luke, about whom the local Jewish leaders said, backing up his request for a cure for his servant:

He is worthy that you should do this, for he loves our nation, and it was he who built us our synagogue. (Luke 7:5)

The goodness of the foreigner is strictly dependent on his attitude with respect to the chosen people. The idea that there might be a goodness independent of what "we" might consider good was then, as it too often is for us, a very odd notion. However it was toward this that Jesus was pointing when he answered the person who asked him if there are many who are saved. This business of the coming of the kingdom works from other criteria, which are not the criteria of any group at all, so that it is possible that those of "our" group have not grasped what it is which makes of a person an heir of the kingdom, while it may indeed have been grasped by people who have nothing to do with this group, people whose way of conceiving goodness seems for those of "our" group either strange or downright despicable.

At the end of the apostolic witness, once again with attention fixed on the slaughtered lamb, we read this:

Thou art worthy to take the book, and to open the seals thereof, for thou wast slain and hast redeemed us to God by thy blood out of every kindred, and tongue, and people and nation.

(Rev. 5:9)

Just in case we haven't got the message, this quartet of people is repeated again at Revelation 7:9, 13:7, and 14:6. Let's have a look at 7:9:

After this I beheld, and lo, a great multitude, which no man could number, of all nations, and kindreds and people, and tongues, stood before the throne, and before the Lamb, clothed with white robes, and palms in their hands.

That is to say, a simply indispensable part of the vision of the open heaven with the risen victim is that around the victim there should be people of every race and nation and people and tongue.

Well now, what relation does the presence of the people of this quartet have with the slaughtered lamb, the victim seated at the right hand of the Father? There is a certain way of treating the passage from Judaism to Christianity which suggests that Judaism was a religion of rites and sacred places, requiring circumcision and the observance of a whole series of laws, and that God no longer wanted anything to do with all that, and so Jesus was sent to teach a religion of interiority and grace, teaching that now the Father is to be worshipped in Spirit and in Truth, reducing all that went before to the commandment of love. From that moment onward there has been no real need for anything that is exterior and visible in religion. And of course, an interior and invisible religion can be lived by people of any race, people, nation, or tongue. The universality of the Church would be owed to God having decreed that now He is universally accessible and has nothing to do with a chosen people. Do you buy this package? If you do buy it, I suggest that what you have bought is the religion sometimes called "liberal Protestantism,"[1] which is to be found not only among the children of the Reformation, but within the Catholic Church, and even under cassocks and religious habits which seem to suggest that their wearers attribute some importance to the exterior and visible element of religion.

What I am going to propose to you is that this model of understanding the passage from Judaism to Christianity is deeply inadequate, natural though it may seem. And this is because it has not understood the relationship between the multitude out of every nation and race and people and tongue, and the slaughtered lamb. We have seen Jesus' prophecy that at the banquet there will be people from the four winds, and then we looked at what was glimpsed by the Seer of Revelation: that is, the beginning and the end of the process. Now let us look at the midpoint, at the moment when the possibility was opened up that Jesus' prophecy would be fulfilled.

Peter is on the rooftop, praying, when he falls into a trance and sees heaven opened, and out of heaven something comes down which he finds repulsive: a sheet full of every kind of beast, and not exactly

---

1. I was perplexed as to whether or not to use this label. However, having failed to find a better one, I have dared to use it only because of the freedom with which many Christians from the Reformed traditions apply this term to themselves and to their own theological history.

the cuddly ones, since it includes reptiles and all. Three times he is told to kill and eat, and he, as a good Jew, refuses, for the beasts are profane and impure (here we perhaps have a reminder of another triple negation of Peter's). So the voice says to him:

What God has cleansed, do not you call impure. (Acts 10:15)

Peter doesn't understand very well what it's all about, but when he enters Cornelius's house, he gets the point and tells his host:

You know that it is unlawful for a Jew to have dealings with foreigners or enter their houses, but God has shown me not to call any person profane or impure. (Acts 10:28)

Now, this last verse is one of the most important lines in our history, since it is what has enabled that history to happen at all. It is the only occasion which we have on record in which Peter used the power which had been entrusted to him to bind and unbind things in heaven and on earth. He declares as an absolutely binding part of the Christian revelation that no human is to be called impure or profane. With this brief infallible declaration the first pope opens the gates of heaven to the gentiles.

His declaration is even more interesting, because he does not say: "God has revealed to me that there's no such thing as that which is impure or profane," but rather not to *call* any person profane or impure. Maybe this distinction doesn't seem important to you. It does to me, for it suggests that in matters human, reality is not something which is just there, independently of what we think it to be: it is not as though we were to say, for example, that in objective point of fact there is nothing profane or impure, but that there are some people who think that there is, and God is saying that they are wrong. No, what Peter says shows a much more subtle understanding than that. Human *reality is a human linguistic construct,* and we all form part of it by our reception and use of words, by the way in which we speak of others. If we describe someone with a certain terminology, our description is not independent of reality, but forms part of the construction of the reality in question. When we call someone something, we're helping to make that person actually be that thing: "give a dog a bad name. . . . ."

So, for example, it used to be said in the United States that black people were more stupid and lazy than white people, and this position was justified with recourse to a whole series of arguments about the supposed differences between the sort of cranium proper to Caucasian and to African-American people. Nobody denies that, when this was said, black people did not in fact present such brilliant school results and there were not so many black people in responsible and well-remunerated jobs, realities which are only just beginning to be modified. However, and this is the fundamental thing which Peter also saw: the social status of black people *is a human linguistic construction*. And what is said about them serves as a pretext to justify a whole series of separations and discriminations which may be economically convenient for a whole lot of people, but corresponds to no reality at all about some supposed essential difference between black and white people. The difference is created artificially by language and believed as much by black as by white, for the former, before the black consciousness movements, tended to introject into themselves the hatred masked by the separatist language, to consider themselves inferior, not beautiful, not intelligent, and so on. The creation in many cultures of a category of impurity for women, taking as its basis the undeniable biological fact of menstruation, and going on from there to posit a supposedly objective foundation for the discrimination produced by the ever-present ambivalence and insecurity of males with relation to women, partakes of exactly the same mechanism.

What Peter is saying when he affirms that God has revealed to him not to call anyone profane or impure is that the heavenly counter-history, the subversion from within of the story of this world, has an indispensable grammatical rule: that no discrimination against any sort of repugnant person can resist the crucible of learning not to call them profane or impure. The story of heaven is the story of how we learn not to call anyone profane or impure, so that a story is created in which there are, in fact, no impure or profane people, where not even disgusting people consider themselves disgusting, but rather where we have learned to disbelieve, and to help them to disbelieve, in their own repugnancy. I keep to words like "disgusting" because it seems to me more useful for our understanding: what Peter saw in his vision seemed to him to be disgusting, and it was so unnecessarily. Our question as we receive the eschatological imagination must be: who are, for me, the repugnant beasts, or for whom am I a repugnant beast? In this way we'll be able to begin to knock down the same wall as Peter.

How then is this vision of the beast-filled sheet coming down out of the open heaven related to the vision of the Son of man seated at the right hand of God? That is exactly the same question as the one about the link between the life, death, and resurrection of Jesus and the coming into existence of the possibility of a universal access to God. In fact, Peter gives us a hint, for he interprets the beasts not in terms of the food which appeared to be their purpose, but as people. He didn't say: God has shown me not to call any food impure. He already knew that, because Jesus had taught it (Mark 7:19). He came to understand that, if no food were impure, much less is any person of whatever kind or degree impure. And more especially, there was a particular impure man who was not. Of course, we're talking about Jesus. The dead and risen Son of man would have been impure in his rôle as an expelled transgressor, and impure as dead. However in fact he was not impure under either of those rubrics, but rather, precisely by having been thrown out, had been constituted mediator of the truth of God.

We can come up to this question from another angle: the angle that was revealed by the innocent victim. Call to mind our original model, which I described in the first chapter, the model of the scapegoat mechanism, the mechanism of the randomly chosen victim, which forms part of mimetic theory. According to this model the group constructs its peace and its goodness by means of the expulsion of someone, or some group, held to be responsible for all the problems and dissensions in the group. The vital element in this construction of group frontiers is that people genuinely believe in the dangerousness of the excluded one. Everyone had to be in agreement about the exclusion, about the unbearable nature of the pollution brought about by that element. They may differ about many things; there may be a great diversity of opinions about other matters, but there is a fundamental agreement about the wickedness of the excluded one. This fundamental agreement is, itself, *a linguistic construction of human reality* over against the expelled one, and it is a self-deceived linguistic construction, which is the same as saying that it is a reality based on a lie, and a violent lie.

What I wanted to suggest is that Jesus' resurrection is at the same time the revelation of that lie: the victim is innocent and is hated without cause. That is to say, the mechanism which founds social order stands exposed, and *for this reason it begins to become impossible to believe in the real blameworthiness of the victim.* However, and here is the problem, if I can no longer believe in the guilt of the victim, then no more can I believe in the linguistic construction of the reality which has given order to my group. That is, if the victim was innocent after all, then all group boundaries are arbitrary and mendacious, all form part of the violent deceit. And if that is true, and those of "our" group are not essentially different from those of any other group, then there is the threat of the collapse of order; the coming about of that which is most feared: absolute lack of differentiation, which means violence out of all control.

There are two possible reactions in the face of the revelation of the innocence of the victim. The first, which is perhaps the most common, is to change victims. That is, we come to see that such and such a person or group is not really dangerous or polluting. But quickly, with a kind of radar antenna, we detect another dangerous group, or person, and repeat the same construction of "our" goodness, cleanness, and purity, by contrast with this other group. When I quoted to you the remarks of the cardinal archbishop of Buenos Aires, we were talking about something similar. He made his call for the obligatory segregation of the gay population *on the same day* that he presided, in the presence of the chief rabbi of Argentina, at a large public Mass of reparation for a bomb explosion at a Jewish center. It didn't seem to have occurred to him that this capacity to fraternize with Jews, especially during a Mass, would have been utterly repugnant to many of his predecessors, and the fraternity became possible thanks to the fact that the size of the murderous expulsion which was the holocaust revealed the lie in an unimaginable way. Before the holocaust, few would have been surprised to hear a cardinal archbishop demanding that the *Jewish* population be confined to a ghetto, and it was in fact common practice in many countries for centuries. Now we can fraternize with the Jews and prescribe the same medicine which used to be prescribed for them, the sending to the ghetto of the semi-different, but apply it to some other group. This is the reaction of someone who changes instruments but carries on playing the same old tune.

The second reaction is the one we see in the case of Peter: that of understanding that the resurrection of the crucified victim does not reveal a particular case of injustice, but the whole founding mechanism of social order. That is, it is not the declaration that, from now on, a certain class of people, previously considered impure, will be considered acceptable, but rather that the whole mechanism which creates impure or profane people of any category will now be deliberately dismantled. And this is very radical, much more radical than it might seem at first sight. This is because, if it is true that what the risen victim reveals is the lie at the heart of the social order that is built over against, or by contrast with, some other, then it is the excluded one who defines me as good by contrast with him or her. It is the existence of the prostitute that makes the Pharisee feel good about himself. If there were no evil, impure people, who would give me my sense of goodness, my security? This question is too evident in the world after the cold war: it was the enemy twin who made us feel safe. Now who are the goodies and who the baddies? Apparently the worst favor you can do to someone is to take away the crutch furnished them by their enemy twin.

Now, here we have something fundamental. Peter's phrase:

God has shown me not to call any person profane or impure.
(Acts 10:28)

might be interpreted as merely removing the crutch, unmasking the violence without leaving anything in its place, which would be a no less catastrophic form of violence. It is very easy to carry out an analysis based on suspicion to show what "is really going on" behind such and such a social form; it is very easy to detect violence, but this can itself be done violently, in which case one is locked into the same violent argument which gets nowhere. But what Peter says suggests something rather different: it is not only a revelation of the murderous mendacity of any form of social separation, but an impetus to construct something different. *Not calling* anyone profane or impure is actually a positive command about building something (as Peter then shows by baptizing Cornelius), not merely an instruction to abstain from a certain form of behavior.

When we describe the collapse of group frontiers we are describing the collapse of the sacred, for the sacred in human cultures *is* disguised violence. And if we were to carry on with the model of change which I tremulously called "liberal Protestant," we would see Christianity as quite simply a force for secularization, which tends to introduce a certain disbelief in the sacredness of human differences established by violence. There are many modern interpretations which see Christianity simply in this light: as the secularizing force *par excellence*. Of course, if we follow on in that vein, then the Church makes no sense, except as a force which has misunderstood the Christian revelation and which is effectively acting as a shock-absorber against the impact of secularization, that is, as something which strives to hold back or brake the process of secularization, but which is on the side of the violent sacred. It would be useless to deny that, in fact, this understanding of the Church has been current, both on the part of those hostile to it and on that of many of its faithful children. The Protestant critique of the Catholic Church from the Reformation onward conceived it as the Antichrist, the way of keeping alive the forms of the ancient Roman empire, opposed at every step to what was truly of the Gospel: what was truly of the Gospel would destroy the sacred, revealing it for the myth that it is. And of course there's no shortage of representatives of the Church (and, nowadays, of Protestants, and others who share the same principles) who have considered their task exactly as a struggle against the secularization which grows and spreads on all sides, taking seriously the duty of shoring up, until the bitter end, the sacred, sacred differences, conceived as things which are of God.

We will see once again that both this critique in favor of secularization and its opposite, the attempt to shore up or restore the sacred, miss the mark. The critique which I have called, for want of a more convenient label, "liberal Protestant" is right to perceive that, on a social level, the tendency of the Christian revelation is to produce a certain secularization, precisely because it produces a disbelief in the guilt of victims. The world seems more sacred, more religious, closer to God, fuller of faith, if, from time to time, we burn witches, because burning witches means that people believe in the efficacy of their arts, in the much-to-be-feared presence of the devil and of other such invisible realities. However, as the Christian revelation advances, people come no longer to believe in the guilt of witches, but rather come to perceive that what leads to their deaths are certain social mechanisms to which certain ugly old ladies fall victim. The old ladies may of course be somewhat perturbed and themselves introject the belief, thinking themselves really to be witches. The question is whether what Jesus came to inaugurate corresponds exactly with its sociologically visible consequences, that is, whether what Jesus wanted was, simply, to do away with the sacred.

On the other hand, the certain Catholicism which I have described, along with its traveling companions, are right to believe that Jesus didn't come merely to abolish the sacred, but that his mission was itself sacred, and that he did not come merely to unleash the forces of human violence which had previously remained disguised, functioning modestly in such a way that for many people, most of the time, there was a certain social harmony, thanks precisely to their mechanisms of expulsion and of order. In fact Jesus did come to bring about something sacred, proceeding from God, and was not a simple secularizer. The question is whether this "certain Catholicism" does not tend to link too closely that which is sacred in the order of this world, whose secret is the murderous lie, with the sacred which Jesus sought to bring about.

You will have realized, of course, that, once again, we're dealing with the two tendencies opposed to the principle of analogy: either the heavenly story has nothing to do with the story of this world, and because of that the Gospel essentially has the function of razing this latter story to the ground; or, on the other hand, there is too close an identification between the heavenly and the earthly stories, with the result that we remain trapped in our violence. Now, I would like to suggest that Jesus did indeed come to create something sacred, that this sacred something is the subversion from within of the traditional sacred and is a positive and creative construction of the sacred. However it is a non-violent sacred.

To see this, let us return to Peter and his vision: the revelation not to *call* any person profane or impure works at the same time as an agent of secularization, pulling down the frontiers not only of Judaism but of all cultures, for every group maintains its frontiers in similar ways. However this instruction not to *call* also works as a rule of grammar for the building of a new sacred order, the order which is built *without victims*, in flexible imitation of the self-giving of the heavenly victim. That is to say, the task of not calling anyone profane or impure obliges us to the subversion from within of *every* human culture and society, risking the wrath of the threatened frontiers in order to un-cover, dis-cover, the innocence of the victim. That is to say, the kingdom comes not as a bulldozing universal force of secularization, but as the task of building, on every violent frontier, a little tale of the overcoming of the particularity of the group, by recovering its victims. In this way there is, in fact, being produced a new sort of sacred, the non-violent sacred, the true sacred which was first put before our eyes by the impure corpse of a dead "transgressor," and which is the definitive un-throning and relocation of all the violent sacred. It is for this reason that in the vision of the new Jerusalem which we saw in the last chapter there is no temple: the order of sacred violence has passed away. In place of the temple there is the slaughtered lamb: not less, but much more, sacred than the temple, for through it God's light flows unhindered.

What I'm trying to say with all this is that the vision of the open heaven and of the slaughtered lamb includes, *as an intrinsic part of the vision,* people of every race, tribe, nation, and tongue, who have washed white their garments in the blood of the lamb. That is, the universality, what we call the catholicity, of what Jesus came to bring about is an indispensable part of the eschatological imagination, and it is so not as a decree of universality, but because the task of the construction of the kingdom, in flexible imitation of Jesus, bears with it the absolute need to build a multitude of particular stories of the overcoming of violent particularity: the adorers of the lamb taken from out of every nation had not merely received their garments, but in every case they had washed them in the blood of the lamb. Those who have their eyes fixed on the open heaven are empowered not merely to stand by and watch the slow secularization of human culture; that is for the birds who take advantage of the mustard bush that they would themselves have eaten if they had found it as seed. Those who have their eyes fixed are writing with their lives the story of the coming into being of an unimagined catholicity, summoned out of all local particularities, around the risen cadaver of the self-giving victim. And this is the great secret of catholicity: while every local culture tends to build its frontiers by means of victims, it is only if we begin from the forgiving victim that we can build a culture which has no frontiers, because we no longer have to build any order, security, or identity *over against some excluded person,* but the excluded one himself gives the identity by allowing us to share in the gratuity of his self-giving.

This can also be understood exactly as part of our vision of the slow pruning of violence from God. As it comes to be seen that God is without violence, then God has nothing to do with the shoring up of sacred frontiers of exclusion, which are part of the same violent mechanism that took Jesus to his death. It was their grasping this which obliged the first Christians to the huge and extraordinary change of cultural mentality which led them to understand that God had indeed chosen the people of Israel, not so that they should forge their identity over against other cultures, but so that God might be revealed as God is, as victim, through them. It was the particular story of Israel which made it humanly possible to come to an understanding that God is among us as someone whom we lynch, the slow working out of that particular story of the subversion from within of the surrounding myths and stories. As it came to be evident that *even Israel* lynches God, then it became clear that God has nothing to do even with the sacred frontiers of Israel, and God called some Jews to take this new perception of God, which could only have come into being thanks to centuries of Jewish history, outside the frontiers of Israel, opening up the possibility of a universal access to God through the self-giving victim.

If all of this seems to have taken us very far from the texts of the apostolic witness, then I would ask you to consider one of the shake-ups to the imagination which Jesus left us in one of his parables. There is a story told by Jesus in which all the elements which I have sketched out here are present: the pure, the impure, a disgusting foreigner, a subversion from within of the understanding of goodness, the relocation of the sacred, the collapse of group frontiers, and a victim. And, if that were not enough, the parable is to be found in Luke. I'm thinking, of course, of the parable of the good Samaritan (Luke 10:25–37). Consider that story in the light of what you've just read: allow its own elements to subvert your imagination. Wherever that story is told, it empowers our eschatological imagination for the arduous construction of catholicity. The inner dynamic between this parable, Peter's declaration, and what the Seer of the Apocalypse saw is seamless.

Redeeming the Time...

The last of the rules of grammar giving us a way into the eschatological imagination which we are going to examine is that of time. This is a rather difficult one to grasp, and I'm not going to do more than sketch out some suggestions with respect to where a more detailed study might lead us.

I've been suggesting that the presence to the apostolic group of the risen victim turned inside-out their conception of God and at the same time revealed that the human condition is so shot through by death that we are incapable of acceding, off our own bats, to God's effervescent and creative aliveness. It was about this we were speaking when we looked at the condition of being "greatly mistaken." I suggested that our whole human condition is formed by the social "other" which precedes us and which is what has enabled us to become socialized humans at all, and also that this social "other" is founded in the murderous lie, which flows from death and tends to produce death.

This means that the whole of human cultural reality, that is, everything which forms us, participates in this fatal tendency. There is no part which escapes. And one of the cultural dimensions which forms us is time. This is absolutely clear the moment we consider that our whole conception of time is of something which has an end. For us time is an ambiguous reality, because just as it is in time that things are born, grow, and develop, so also in time things grind down, decompose, and pass, or, in the case of living things, die. Even the Andes, in whose radiant shade these lines are being written, are in movement, passing from one state to another. It forms no part of our consciousness, of that which allows us to be conscious at all, that things might have no end. Normally we do not even stop to think about such things, so obvious does it seem to us that time is a continuous movement of growth and decay, with our own lives as paradigmatic examples. Even without the intervention of violent forces from without, we observe the process by which we grow, and, from a certain age, begin to pass, or decline, toward death.

When Jesus, then, created for us a *belief,* that is, when he went to his death as if death were not, with his imagination absolutely fixed on the God who has nothing to do with death, a quite extraordinary element is introduced into the understanding of time, and that is the possibility of a mode of time which has no end. It seems to me that for us to understand this it is necessary once again for us to have recourse to the later texts of the apostolic witness. John speaks to us frequently of *zoé aiōnios,* which we usually translate as "eternal life." Perhaps it would be more useful to translate the phrase as "life without end," for "eternal" means "without time," that is, it qualifies something which has neither beginning nor end, properly speaking only God, for we do indeed begin: there was when we were not. However the interesting thing is that the possibility is being adumbrated of our living in a way that has no end. Here it is worthwhile saying that the important part of the phrase "life without end" is the word "life." "Without end" is a way of pointing to the abundance of life which we receive when we allow ourselves to be re-created by God.

Another way of saying the same thing is by pointing out that the belief which Jesus inaugurated when he enabled us to live as if death were not also enables us to live as if there were no end. That is, we can start here to construct something, a life story, which has no end. But this introduces into human history something quite extraordinary: the possibility of a story which is only one of growth, of coming into existence, of development, and which is in no way shaded by its contrary. And this, logically enough, tends to relativize the time which we all know and live normally, the ambiguous time where we grow and decay. It means that two different qualities of time co-exist: the time of that which is coming into existence, which has no end, and the time which is subject to human violence, a time by means of which we seek our security, fortifying ourselves, grasping our existence in a struggle against the universal tendency to pass away.

What I would like to suggest to you is that the pruning away of violence from the perception of God, the process we have already seen, is *exactly at the same time* the coming into existence of a quality of time which knows no violence. Time which is a gift for building, and not time which must be grasped for survival. We have evidence in the apostolic witness of this process of pruning time of its violence, until an understanding was reached of the simultaneity of the two qualities of time: the one without end, and the other vain and futile. I suggest to you that the whole discussion in the apostolic witness about the end, the delay, the day, and the coming of the Son of man, is exactly related to this theme.

We will look more closely at these questions when we finally get around to more strictly eschatological matters in our remaining chapters. For now I propose to you the slightly arduous task of examining how we relate to time. We can make a division between physical time, which we measure in seconds, minutes, and so on, and psychological time, that is, our appreciation of time. No one finds it strange that there should be a difference between these two, for we all have the experience of when we were little, and time seemed to pass so much more slowly: a year, the time between birthday parties or Christmas presents, seemed to last an eternity. As we get older we have the impression of time accelerating: if I ask what it was that I was doing this time last year, the interval seems to have flown by.

Well, the key to psychological time is our memory. That is, we were introduced into psychological time in the degree to which, as we grew, our memory was constituted. This memory is produced in us principally by imitation. It is as we learn to imitate sounds and gestures that we begin to be able to receive and to tell a story: exactly the same process by which we come to have an identity. In fact it is our memory which enables us to be individuals at all, the person who tells this story. Someone without a memory not only does not know what happened in the past, but quite literally does not know who he or she is: that is what happens in grave cases of amnesia.

Another example of the way in which physical and psychological time are two separate realities is offered by what happens in hypnosis. Let us imagine that I am a hypnotist, and I hypnotize Mercedes.

What the hypnotist does is to distract Mercedes' conscious attention and suggest into existence a new "person"; let's call her Mercedes 2. I tell Mercedes 2 to learn by heart a list of Greek verbs, and she does just that — let us suppose that she had never learned Greek before. For as long as Mercedes 2 is functioning, that is, during the hypnotic trance, Mercedes 2 has a perfect memory of what she was doing before hypnosis. All her memories of youth are intact, her participation in the recent history of her country, her adolescent passions, and so on. That is, Mercedes 2 remembers Mercedes 1 perfectly well. Now, the moment I take Mercedes out of her hypnotic trance, she will carry on remembering all that happened to her before I hypnotized her, but she will have no memory at all of having learned Greek, nor of anything else that happened to her while Mercedes 2 was functioning.

This means something very interesting: for Mercedes 1, now fully awake, Mercedes 2 is not in her past, nor in her present, nor in her future, but in another time not accessible to her. In terms of physical time, Mercedes 2 was in the past of Mercedes 1, because I hypnotized her between, let us say, ten and eleven this morning, and it is now, let us say, two in the afternoon. In terms of psychological time, Mercedes 2 forms no part at all of Mercedes 1, because the hypnotist had suggested into existence, by means of imitative desire (which is the secret of hypnosis) a new "persona" (fairly short-lived of course). All this is of immense interest from a theological point of view, because it gives us a certain idea about how God calls into existence a new person, how he creates the person we are going to be, inducing in us a pacific imitation of a way of being human which reforms us completely from within. But that is not what I want to deal with now.

The important thing for now is the rôle of memory. Hypnosis works because someone allows someone else to suggest them into existence. That is to say, it requires a pacific and trusting handing-over to what the other person will do with "me." What I would like to suggest is that our initial being suggested into existence, through our home, our relatives, and so on, functions by exactly the same mechanism. That is, the "other," which is previous to us, suggests us by its desires into existence, by giving us desires, gestures, words, and then stories, within which we learn to inscribe ourselves. That is, the whole process by which we come to be a person works by something equivalent to a socialized hypnosis. The little hypnotic trance we imagined is nothing exceptional, just an absolutely normal process conducted by a qualified individual under laboratory conditions. If you want to see exactly the same phenomenon outside laboratory conditions, I suggest that you study those old documentary films of Hitler's speeches before massed crowds. Even those who don't understand a word of German, and perhaps especially those of us who don't, and so are not distracted by the contents of the speeches, can see that the Führer was capable of producing a collective hypnosis in which people could lose their identity and come to form part of a collective person, ready for any barbarism. The mechanism is the same.

If in fact we are formed in this way, if our person is called into being in this way from our tenderest infancy, then we must observe that, by contrast with what happens in a limited session of hypnosis where there is a trusting handing-over through a pacific imitation, the story of our initial being called into existence was not pacific. Conflicting desires were suggested to us, and elements of rivalry were introduced into the formation of our "I," that is, into what allows us to have an "I" at all, in such a way that we learn to build our identity in a rivalistic way, simultaneously being suggested into existence and forgetting what we owe the "other," and denying it. That is to say, our identity is, in all our cases, half-received, half-grasped. And our way of grasping our identity is precisely by introducing distortions into our memory. This is seen very clearly in striking cases where, for example, a girl has been abused by her father at a tender age and reacts by blocking out the memory completely, perhaps recovering it many years later with much difficulty and pain. Often in these cases such people do not know until the recovery of the memory why they have certain compulsive forms of behavior, or why they are missing a whole lot of feelings that other people seem to have.

The less harsh forms of the same mechanism are universal, but function in exactly the same way. That is to say that we build our identity both by receiving the identity which is given to us by what is other than us and, at the same time, by erecting frontiers of negation of our dependence on that other. And it is not simply that we are, ourselves, reacting against something like an invasion from outside, as though there were an original "I" within and hostile elements without, but rather that *the sort of desire which we receive from the other already includes elements of rejection and ambivalence.* That is, everything that enables me to have an "I" already includes these elements of rejection and denial. By saying this I am not saying anything other than what the Church has always said when it affirms that the whole person is, from conception, and in every case, formed from within by "Original Sin."

What I would like to suggest is that this way of ours of receiving identity, which comes half-received, half-grasped, participates in exactly the same mechanism which we have seen to underlie the formation of group boundaries, that is: the mechanism of the randomly chosen victim. I learn to define myself *over against* some other, making a contrast with that other in order to give myself security and identity. In this way I grasp my identity, which comes to birth as a function of what is rejected and denied. This also happens in the social group which seeks to leave behind the terrible threat of a violent loss of differences, where there seem to be no laws, by looking for some person, or group, over against whom to define itself, that is, by expelling someone, and, from the starting point of this expulsion defining, for its own internal consumption, what is good and bad, what pure and impure, and so on.

The similarity, or rather, identity, between the process of social formation and the process in the formation of the person doesn't stop there. You will remember that a fundamental part of the mechanism of the randomly chosen victim is the fact that the persecutors really believe their victim to be guilty and, having expelled the victim, tell the story of what happened, from their own perspective of course, not perceiving the arbitrariness of their action and the innocence of their victim. This means that the story which they tell is a deceitful memory of what in fact happened, and by means of this deceitful and lying memory, they create and constitute their identity as a group and their group frontiers.

Well, we each do exactly the same thing: in every case our memory exercises the function of a deceitful story with respect to what really happened. And our identity and our boundaries as a person are kept up by means of this lie, or myth, which also leads us into a whole series of repetitive and compulsive behaviors, which students of psychology do not hesitate to call "ritualistic."

Now our relationship with time, psychological time, depends exactly on memory. In the degree to which our memory is false, insisting on the originality of what is "mine" and denying or altering the dependence on the other which in fact brought me to existence, our person is constituted by a denial of physical time, that is, of the real movement of what happened, and we are in a conflictual relationship with time. Time has to be grasped for us to give ourselves worth, for we have to protect ourselves against time. And this for a fundamental reason: our projection toward the future depends entirely on our relationship with the past. Where we distort our relationship with the past, our future has to be something against which we must protect ourselves.

This means that time, for us, formed in the murderous lie, comes from death (the truth hidden by the deceitful memory) and tends toward death: the future is death, against the truth of which we protected ourselves in the past and against whose reality in the future we seek to protect ourselves by grasping and seizing our vain identity, our futile security. But this means that our relationship with the past and with the future is exactly the same relationship, and that for us the notion of time is always marked by the notion of "end," which means "death" in a way that is not only physical but also psychological. It is for this reason that the notion of the eternal return, which Nietzsche went back to teaching, is typical of pagan religion, for it is a question of a recurring cycle from death to death: an ideologized version of the compulsively ritualistic behavior which accompanies the living out of the lie, the mendacious memory.

Now, and here we have what is important, the vision which we have in the apostolic witness of the risen victim who opens up the mediation of God alludes simultaneously to the past and to the future. If we practice the *memory* of the self-giving of the forgiving victim ("Do this in memory of me"), then we are empowered to have our memory unbound from its deceit, we can see and accept and remain free from our mendacious self-construction of the past, our lie is revealed to us as something capable of being forgiven, which *also and simultaneously* allows us to imagine a future which has no end. I suggest to you that the instruction "Do this in memory of me" and the exhortation "Fix your mind on the things that are above...where Christ is seated at the right hand of God" are exactly the same instruction: the loving self-giving of the past and the future promise of receiving a full self-giving *are the same thing.*

Let us notice how this works: it is the forgiving victim who enables our memories to be healed. That is, the forgiveness of sins and the healing of memories is the same thing: what unbinds our past is what opens up our future.

Please excuse the difficulty of all this, but it is of great importance if we are to understand the birth of the possibility of "eternal life" or life without end. The revelation of God which Jesus brought about, the God who is known from the risen victim, made it possible that, instead of the constitution of a person whose memory is bound up in expulsive grasping of being because of the violent "other" which surrounds him and gives him birth, the "Other" which brings us to existence might be perfectly without violence, without rivalry. This revelation makes it possible for our memory, and through it, our life-story and our person, to be called into existence in such a way that the memory and the past do not form a threatening present, but rather a present which is in a process of constant enrichment by what is being given it, and where the future is precisely the continuation of an ever greater and ever richer reception of life. I think that when, in John's Gospel, Jesus says that he came so that we might have life and have it *abundantly* (John 10:10), it is the same thing as when he refers to "eternal" life, life without end.

All this has as its object one thing alone, which is to try to demonstrate, from a certain anthropological starting point, why there is to be found in the apostolic witness a change in the notion of time. What we find is, on the one hand, the coming into existence of a time that is capable of redemption, human time transformed into a time capable of participating in the endless abundance of God's life, and, on the other hand, evil, futile time, which is passing away and which leads only to dissolution and to death. This change in the conception of the quality of time is absolutely and rigorously dependent on the revelation of the completely radiant vivaciousness and lovingkindness of the Father made available by the risen victim and is part of the complete coherence of the development of that revelation. I think that here we come to understand something of the density of the phrase which we find in the epistle to the Ephesians:

> See then that ye walk circumspectly, not as fools but as wise, redeeming the time, because the days are evil. (Eph. 5:15–16)

Here the two qualities of time which we have seen are both present: time capable of redemption and evil time, that is, time capable of participating in a life which has no end and a time bound to grasping onto repetitions seeking to avoid an always-to-be-feared end.

With this we have, I think, the necessary elements with which to focus in the remaining chapters on a series of more specifically eschatological questions, to see where they lead us.

The Apocalyptic Imagination and the Delayed Parousia

In our last chapter we examined two realities which form part of the process by which Jesus' creative imagination came to possess the apostolic group: how the universality of salvation came to be possible, and how it came to be possible to imagine time in a way that has no end. We saw the difference made both to the world of group frontiers and to that of time which is born and passes away by the vision of the heavens open around the risen victim. I hope that with this preparation we have reached the end of the introductory part of this study, of my attempt to lay the foundations for an examination of certain properly eschatological themes. Remember our starting point in the verse:

> Fix your minds on the things that are above... (Col. 3:2)

and how this verse relates to Jesus' Ascension. You will have become aware that it is the Ascension, that is heaven open with the risen victim seated at the right hand of God, which is the pivotal point for trying to recover the eschatological imagination. That vision underlies everything which follows.

A Problem of Interpretation: Jesus Gets It Wrong?

When we read the texts of the apostolic witness we find a whole series of signs which are capable of the following interpretation: Jesus preached the imminent arrival of the kingdom of God, which would include his own return from the dead in glory and the beginnings of a judgment in the exercise of which he would be helped by the twelve apostles, the symbolic Israel. He had promised the disciples that they would not die before seeing this, his arrival in glory, which would vindicate all the sufferings of his followers. The problem was that the years began to pass after the resurrection, and there was no sign of a glorious return, nor of a beginning of judgment. The Temple was destroyed as Jesus had predicted, but no hint of the arrival of a restored Temple. The early preaching of the apostles included this element of the imminent arrival of the Lord in glory, and, when this didn't materialize, the early Christians entered into doubt about what really was to happen, with the result that the apostolic writers found themselves having to sweeten the pill, creating some more or less mythological explanations which would allow for the postponement of Jesus' arrival. In fact, it was this process of postponing the coming which obliged Christians to organize their lives on a long-term basis and which led to the setting up of what has been called, in good German theological jargon, *Frühkatholizismus,* or primitive Catholicism, with its incipient Church structure and hierarchy.

This primitive Catholicism was, on the one hand, the fruit of Jesus getting it wrong: he would never have wanted it, because he intended to come back in glory before such a thing could have developed, and anyhow he had been interested in some sort of mysterious restoration of Israel and its Temple. On the other hand, the coming about of *Frühkatholizismus* was the result of the efforts of the apostolic group to do the best they could, given the need to invent a way of compensating those who had believed them for the non-fulfillment of their hope. The end of this process might be detected in John's Gospel, where there is no longer any insistence on hope nor a looking to the future, but where everything has been absorbed in a timeless promise of eternal life, so as to produce a Gospel which would stand up to the non-arrival of what had previously been awaited.

You very probably recognize this explanation and have heard it before. Various elements of the liberal Protestant soil which gave it birth can be detected, like the belief that the arrival of the Catholic Church was a very early perversion of the original Gospel message of Jesus, who would have wanted no such thing. Also there is the belief that it was the apostles, and not Jesus, who founded the Church (which would mean that there are no sacraments of Christ, but only of the Church, and thus that the whole hierarchical structure of the Church is simply a human invention and is an obstacle to Jesus' message rather than something capable of mediating it). All these arguments were born at the time of the Reformation and turn up in a different form in every generation, within the Catholic Church[1] and outside it.

However, there is a further element to this vision which is, as I see it, rather more worrying. This is the fact of imagining that, when it comes down to it, the apostolic group was acting in bad faith. According to this view they quite clearly understood Jesus, realized after a certain time that he was deceived, and rather than renounce the task of spreading the Gospel when they understood their mistake, they falsified his message, creating something quite different from what Jesus would have wanted. However the greatest problem lies *not* in saying that, in fact, the Church was founded by people rather like the Grand Inquisitor in Dostoyevsky's exceptionally penetrating parable in *The Brothers Karamazov,* that is, by people who were holding back the strength of the Gospel rather than transmitting it. It lies in not believing the apostolic witnesses: in accusing them of willful deceit. The problem is that we have no access to what Jesus thought he was doing except through the witness of the apostolic group, and if we don't believe them about that, why believe anything they say at all? This is the fundamental problem, a question of logic: either you believe them or you don't. But to say that they were telling the truth here and here, but not there and there, presupposes that we have some other access to the truth about Jesus which does not depend on their witness, and this supposed other point of access simply does not exist. That is to say, there is a big logical problem at the root of the interpretation of the delay in the coming of the Son of man.

Leaving this aside for the moment, let us look through the texts which apparently give backing to the view which I described to you, calling it, for want of a better term, "liberal Protestant." That is to say, we're going to look at very early texts which seem to take for granted an imminent return of Jesus in glory, and then the later texts where this vision is toned down and the Parousia of the Son of man seems to be postponed.

We will begin with some of the earliest texts of the apostolic witness, which are to be found in the epistles to the Thessalonians:

For this we say unto you by the word of the Lord, that we which are alive and remain unto the coming of the Lord shall

---

1. The central essay and thesis in L. Boff's controversial work *Church: Charism and Power* (New York: Crossroad, 1986) is a reworking of some of these themes, and it was this, rather than any supposed social radicalism, which was the principal subject of the strictures of the Congregation for the Doctrine of the Faith against his teaching.

not go before them which are asleep. For the Lord himself shall descend from heaven with a shout, with the voice of the archangel, and with the trump of God: and the dead in Christ shall rise first: then we which are alive and remain shall be caught up together with them in the clouds to meet the Lord in the air: and so shall we ever be with the Lord. . . . But of the times and the seasons, brethren, ye have no need that I write unto you. For you yourselves know perfectly that the day of the Lord so cometh as a thief in the night. For when they shall say, Peace and safety: then sudden destruction cometh upon them, as travail upon a woman with child; and they shall not escape.

(1 Thess. 4:15–17; 5:1–3)

In the second epistle to the Thessalonians we read that it will be:

. . . a righteous thing with God to recompense tribulation to them that trouble you; and to you who are troubled rest with us, when the Lord Jesus shall be revealed from heaven with his mighty angels, *In flaming fire taking vengeance on them that know not God,* and that obey not the Gospel of our Lord Jesus Christ. (2 Thess. 1:6–8, with quote from Isa. 66:15 in italics)

Paul then goes on to correct some interpretations current among the Thessalonians with respect to the coming: that they should not be

shaken by supposed revelations, sayings or letters from us as if we were affirming that the day of the Lord is at hand. . . . First must come the apostasy and the appearance of iniquity in person, the man destined to perdition. . . . Do you not remember that while I was still with you I told of these things? You know what now holds him back, so that his appearance happens at the proper time. Because this hidden iniquity is already at work: scarcely will there be taken out of the way the one who for now holds him back when the impious one will appear, whom the Lord *shall consume with the breath of his mouth* and destroy with the splendor of his coming. (2 Thess. 2:2–8 with quote from Isa. 11:4 and Ps. 33:6 in italics)

We could multiply passages like these. Let us concentrate only on those which refer to the day as coming like a thief in the night, for it is clear that this comparison of the coming with a thief goes right back to Jesus. It is to be found in the Gospels of Matthew (24:42–44) and Luke (12:39–40). We have seen that Paul refers to the phrase as already known to his audience, presumably because it was a word of the Lord. It is also to be found in 2 Peter (3:10), and even in Revelation (16:15), where it also appears as a word of the Lord.

Now it is quite clear that the concept of "that day" is transformed during the first century. Even within the writings of Paul such a change can be detected. Look at this from 1 Corinthians, written after 1 Thessalonians:

> Now if anyone build upon this foundation (which is Christ) with gold, silver, precious stones, wood, hay, stubble the work of each one shall be made manifest: for the day shall manifest it when it is revealed in fire. And the fire will try the quality of the work of each one. That one whose work, built on the foundation, stands up will receive a reward. But the one whose work is burned up will suffer loss. He, however, will be saved, but as one who passes through fire. (1 Cor. 3:12–15)

So now the day doesn't receive emphasis as "a moment of time" but as a principle that will reveal a certain continuity between this world and the next. The relationship between the day and the fire is subtly different from the relationship in 1 and 2 Thessalonians.

In the same letter to the Corinthians we also read that:

> the time is growing short [*sunestalmenos esti*] (1 Cor. 7:29)

but now, rather than this being a threat concerning the proximity of the end, the concept of "time" is suffering a change, for, as a result of the time which is growing short, Paul recommends to his audience a special behavior, enjoying as if they did not enjoy, possessing as if they did not possess, and so on

> because the form of this world is passing away...
> (1 Cor. 7:31)

That is to say, the quality of the time begins to be linked with a certain way of behaving in the "here and now." In the same letter Paul shows that he has had more time to think about the relationship between this world and the one to come, and he gives a somewhat different vision from what he had given in his Thessalonian correspondence. There is no longer that element of "rapture" (being seized away, like the celestial rape which Zeus is said to have practiced on

Ganymede), but in its place, transformation in an instant. Now Paul is able to explain the different forms of bodiliness which correspond to each world: the mortal and corruptible form, and that which is incorruptible and deathless (see 1 Cor. 15:35–58).

Well, if we move on to 2 Peter, a much later text, we see that the same concepts are dealt with in a quite different manner:

> In the last days will come those who will scoff at everything and act according to their own desires. They will ask: "what has become of the promise of his coming?..." but do not forget one thing, friends: that for the Lord a day is like a thousand years and a thousand years like a day. The Lord does not delay what he promised, even though some count it so; but he has patience with us because he does not want anyone to perish, but that everyone should have room to change heart. The day of the Lord will indeed come like a thief, and then the heavens will pass away with a great noise, and the elements will melt with fervent heat, and the earth and what is upon it shall disappear.... Nevertheless we, according to his promise, look for *new heavens and a new earth* where righteousness dwell. (2 Pet. 3:3–4a, 8–10, 13 with quote from Isa. 65:17 and 66:22 in italics)

The author recognizes that there are people for whom the delay is a cause of stumbling and seeks to explain the matter by recourse to biblical metaphysics, that is, an explanation that our concept of time is not the same as God's, and that this delay, rather than a motive for being scandalized, is a sign of God's mercy: it is time given to allow a change of heart, time in which there is shown the large-heartedness of God who does not want anyone to perish.

When we move to the Gospels we see various signs of an awareness that the delay was something which needed an explanation. In Matthew's Gospel, Jesus, at the end of his "eschatological discourse," speaks of those who have been put in charge of feeding the servants, with evident reference to the leaders of the Church, and says:

> But if that wicked servant says in his heart "My Lord is delaying his coming" and begins to ill-treat his fellow servants and to eat and to drink with the drunken, then on a day that he is not expecting it, and at an hour when he is not looking out for it, his Lord will come.... (Matt. 24:48–50a)

We see the same thing in the Lucan version of the same instruction of the Lord (Luke 12:45). Matthew also gives space to the element of the delay in the parable of the wise and the foolish maidens:

> Since the bridegroom was delayed, they all became drowsy and went to sleep.... (Matt. 25:5)

He does this at the same time as he underlines Jesus' insistence that the reason for the parable is so that people stay awake, for they know neither the day nor the hour (Matt. 25:13). So it is possible to interpret all these phrases as latter additions made by the apostolic group in order to explain away a delay which originally neither Jesus nor they had expected.

Something similar could be attributed to John's interpretation of the Temple. Very early on in that Gospel, Jesus removes the traders from the Temple and predicts its destruction and restoration, and John takes care to point out:

> But the temple he spoke of was his body. When therefore he rose from the dead his disciples remembered that he had said these things, and they believed the Scripture and the word which Jesus had said. (John 2:21–22)

One interpretation of this, following the line which I have sketched out, would be that this displacement of the Temple onto Jesus' body was the way the apostolic group tried to account for an inexplicable delay in the restoration of the Temple, and so laid hold of a metaphorical explanation which would get them off the hook.

We have seen that there is, in fact, an undeniable development in the way of focusing on the coming, the day, the delay, and so on. And we have also seen that there certainly were people who believed that part of what Jesus had promised was his own imminent return in glory, and who were, at the very least, confused by the delay which they were experiencing. However, I wonder whether all this evidence isn't capable of a different interpretation, somewhat more subtle, and much more interesting (because not based on imputing bad faith to the apostolic group), and it is this that I will seek to unfold.

The Apocalyptic Imagination

You will have noticed, on reading the passages which I quoted, and above all those from Thessalonians, that they use a great deal of violent language: the day of vengeance, of punishment, of affliction, and other such expressions. None of this seems to sit well with what I've been trying to set out in previous chapters about the coming about of a perception of God that is pruned of violence. Let us face up to this apparent contradiction. The passages which employ this violent language make use of a literary recourse that was widespread in the eastern Mediterranean at the time of Jesus and is called by its students the "apocalyptic" genre. When we talk of a literary genre we are talking about a way of imagining things that enjoyed a certain popularity, that is, we are talking about an imagination. Now, this literary genre, which had been in development since the late prophetic literature (and which can be found well-developed in, for example, the book of Daniel, as well as in other books which we do not usually have in our Bibles,[2] like those of Esdras), has certain characteristics. Normally there is a heavenly vision, mediated by angels, and the end of this world is promised, along with a consolation of the just, among other things. It was in this ambience that the vision of the resurrection of the Maccabee brothers, which we have already looked at, was born.

According to Wayne Meeks, a student of this subject, the apocalyptic genre, and for that reason, the apocalyptic imagination, is characterized by the presence of certain dualities, which can be characterized as follows:[3] a cosmic dualism, that is, between heaven and earth (with heaven becoming known through visions mediated by angels); a temporal dualism, between this world, or age, and the world, or age, to come, which will begin with the end, probably the destruction, of this one; and a social dualism, that is, a division between the good and the bad, the righteous and the impious, the afflicted and the persecutors. This dualism, which imagined the present distress of the righteous and afflicted, would of course be reversed in the age to

---

2. Different deuterocanonical books are included in what is sometimes called the "apocrypha" by different Churches, with some included and some excluded in the ancient traditions of different Oriental Churches. The matter is well explained in the introduction to the Common Bible, the ecumenical edition of the RSV.

3. See his "Social Functions of Apocalyptic Language in Pauline Christianity," in D. Hellholm, ed., *Apocalypticism in the Mediterranean World and the Near East* (Tübingen, 1983).

come. The language which Paul uses in 1 Thessalonians seems to fit exactly into this explanation.

Now, what vision of God and of time lies behind this imagery? It is clear that we are not looking at a pagan version of the eternal return, that is, a vision which flows from death to death. The Jews knew very well that such an understanding of time is incompatible with belief in the One Living God. They understood full well (and this had come about during the time of the prophets along with the birth of the understanding of human responsibility and of the possibility of choosing between this or that course of action in a particular historical circumstance) that time runs toward a judgment; this conception is only accessible in the degree to which linear time came to be born. What I suggest to you is that the apocalyptic imagination understands this time-running-toward-judgment still within an understanding of a partial God, just toward the righteous, and implacable with the iniquitous, and that the apocalyptic imagery serves as a way of imagining an ultimate eschatological vengeance in favor of those who feel they are victims, those who resent the present order of things. That is, while the apocalyptic imagination is a huge advance over the pagan imagination, it is still stuck within a notion of a violent God.

The question then, is this: when Jesus talked of his coming and of the end, was he simply enclosed within the apocalyptic imagination? That is, did he accept the dualities proper to the apocalyptic imagination as part of what he was preaching and announcing? It will come as no surprise to you if I say that, as I see it, he was not. It seems to me that what we have with Jesus is precisely and deliberately the subversion from within of the apocalyptic imagination. What I have called the eschatological imagination *is nothing other than* the subversion from within of the apocalyptic imagination. That is, Jesus used the language and the imagery which he found around him to say something rather different. There are various ways of glimpsing this in the Gospel, for example, in the contrast which is made between the preaching of John the Baptist, which does indeed fit within the apocalyptic imagination, and that of Jesus. Maybe we can see this better if we draw up to it in an indirect way, that is, Jesus' attitude with respect to the social and the cosmic dualities would already be a good indication of his attitude with respect to the temporal duality.

It is evident that Jesus did not simply accept the social duality of his time, the division between good and evil, pure and impure, Jews and non-Jews. In fact, his practice and his teaching add up to a powerful subversion of this duality. Neither did he accept the cosmic duality, as can be seen in his announcing the coming about *now* of the kingdom of God and, for example, in his teaching his disciples to ask, in their prayer to God:

> Thy will be done on earth as it is in heaven.

His practice of, and teaching about, celibacy lived now for the king-dom of God — for the children of the resurrection neither marry nor are given in marriage — would be another indication of the same thing. So that it would be very surprising if, breaking as he did with the apocalyptic scheme in these areas, we must imagine that his teaching concerning the temporal duality and the coming of the end remained perfectly within the duality which we have seen, leaving it intact.

There is then a good *prima facie* reason for thinking that the sub-version of the apocalyptic imagination by what I have called Jesus' eschatological imagination is something proper to Jesus rather than something invented by a disconcerted early community in the face of the indefinite postponement of the Day. This *prima facie* evidence deepens somewhat when we discover that at the root of the subver-sion which Jesus was making of these dualities, the criterion of the victim is to be found. Jesus offers a prophetic criterion in terms of ethical demands that are capable of being carried out as the basis of his subversion of these dualities: the social duality is redefined in terms of the victim, so that the victim is the criterion for determining if one is a sheep or a goat (Matt. 25), or if one is a neighbor (Luke 10); it is victims and those who live precariously who are to be at the center of the new victim people, to whom belongs the kingdom of God which is arriving (Matt. 5–6). No one can be surprised that this insistence, more in the line of the prophetic imagination than the apocalyptic, comes also to be subversive of the cosmic and temporal dualities. It is thus that the forgiving victim, the crucified and risen one, comes to be, himself, the presence of the kingdom in the here and now.[4]

If we consider it in this light, it doesn't seem surprising that there should have been a development among the members of the apostolic group in the period after the resurrection. If we take the notion of the

---

4. Luke 17:20: "*The kingdom of God is entos humōn*" — among you? In your hands? Between your hands? — As when you hand me over....

"end" understood as vengeance, just as it is found in 1 Thessalonians, it is a vengeful end which depends exactly on there being insiders and outsiders, so that the afflicted are vindicated, and the persecutors punished. But in the degree to which the perception of God changes, becoming, as we have seen, shorn of violence, two realities are altered simultaneously: the separation between goodies and baddies, insiders and outsiders, enters into a process of continuous collapse and subversion, and at the same time the "end" cannot remain as a vengeance if there is no longer any clarity about who's an insider and who's an outsider, and under these circumstances the notion of the end itself changes toward what we see in 2 Peter: it becomes a principle of revelation of what had really been going on during the time that has been left for the changing of hearts. The Matthean parables of the wheat and the tares and of the good and bad fishes which we saw in chapter 4 say exactly the same thing. That is, as God is shorn of violence, *of necessity* a new conception of time is discovered, the time in which the new universality is built. In this way the End, rather than being a vengeful conclusion to time, comes to be a principle, operative in time, by means of which we may live out the arrival of the Son of man, the being alert for the thief in the night, the whole time. We will study this in greater detail when we analyze the eschatological passages from the four Gospels in the next chapter.

For the moment it seems at least acceptable to suggest that the presence among the disciples of the crucified and risen victim is also the principle by which the duality we have seen between this age and the next is subverted, and by means of which a different comprehension of time itself is born. This comprehension, which we looked at in the previous chapter, might be described as that of time capable of participating in eternity, as distinct from time bent away from eternity. Where time is bent away from eternity, there cannot but be a duality of opposition between this age and the next, and the irruption of God into the human story can only be violent, bringing to its end the present age and beginning a new one. However, where the heavenly reality of the crucified and risen victim is already present to the apostolic group, allowing the beginnings of a human life and sociality which are not marked by death, but whose members are free to live a life of self-giving in imitation of Jesus thanks to their faith in the death-less nature of God, then a continuity is already coming about between this age and the next. Human time itself, an unalienable dimension of the physical creatureliness of the human being, has begun to become capable of sharing in life without end.

The Lucan Witness

What I am proposing here is no more than a further aspect of what we have already seen about how the presence to the apostolic group of the crucified and risen Lord knocked down the social duality between Jew and gentile, as is set out in the book of Acts. There is no doubt there about the difficulty of the process by which the universality of the new people was brought into existence by the risen victim. Peter had to be pushed by God into baptizing Cornelius; there were endless conflicts about circumcision; Paul had to fight for years for it to be absolutely clear that there now exists no social duality, thanks to the work of Christ. That is to say, the consequences of what was already embryonically present at Pentecost and in Peter's declaration, which we saw in the last chapter, were not grasped immediately, and the apostolic witness offers evidence of the arduous process by which a truth inherent in the resurrection of the crucified victim came to be "received" or incarnated in the life of the Church. No one now suggests that it was "the weight of reality" (hordes of gentiles forcing their way in, shoving against the Berlin Wall of an obstinate apostolic clinging to a mistaken belief of Jesus that he was sent only to the lost sheep of the house of Israel) which provoked the development from Judaism to Catholicism. The inner coherence between the resurrection and the universality of the new faith has become apparent, however difficult it may have been to perceive it at the beginning.

What I am suggesting is that exactly the same slow and conflictual process by which it came to be understood that what God is calling into existence is universal, without frontiers, is at work in the relationship between the apostolic group and "time." That is to say, there was a big gap before the full force of the consequences of the eschatological imagination which Jesus already had, and which was accessible to the apostolic group starting from the resurrection, was able to carry through the subversion of the prodigious inertia of cultural comprehension (and of the apocalyptic imagination proper to small and threatened groups), and thus enable that eschatological imagination to be received by the Church. Of course, and as we have seen in the apostolic texts, there were Christians, probably many Christians, who did indeed think in terms of the imminent arrival of the End and for whom its delay was a cause of stumbling (just as there were those who thought that all Christians should be circumcised). However, the apostolic teaching about this matter was not the slow justifying of something embarrassing, but the gradual understanding and development of a coherence which was internal to the presence of the crucified and risen victim, accessible through the "mind fixed on the things that are above," part of the irruption into the here and now of the definitive eschatological presence of God and of the new human relationality made possible by this presence.

I do not think that it is by chance that the same author among the apostolic group who most fully sets out the birth of the universal dimension of the new salvation is also the one who gives most hints of the existence of a new notion of time. I'm thinking of Luke. Matthew and Mark could be read as though they were suggesting that Jesus' eschatological discourses referred to what was to happen to Jerusalem, and that after the destruction of the Temple, then the Son would come. In Luke something different is seen. In his vision, Jerusalem is already abandoned by God before its destruction:

O Jerusalem, Jerusalem, which killest the prophets, and stonest them that are sent unto thee; how often would I have gathered thy children together, as a hen doth gather her brood under her wings, and ye would not! Behold your house is left unto you desolate. (Luke 13:34–35a)

Then, when he predicts the destruction of Jerusalem in his eschatological discourse, Jesus adds something very significant:

And they shall fall by the edge of the sword, and shall be led away captive into all nations: and Jerusalem shall be trodden down by the Gentiles, until the time of the Gentiles be fulfilled.
(Luke 21:24)

That is, the whole of Jesus' eschatological discourse referred to this living *in the times of the gentiles,* of the nations. When Jesus describes how people must take heed — how not to meditate upon what they are to say when they are led before tribunals and so on — he is talking about life in the midst of the time which came into being *at the same time as the revelation moved outside the frontiers of Judaism.* The transformation of Israel into "the Israel of God," which comes about through the new creation of a universality without frontiers, is simultaneous with the creation of a new quality of time.

Following this reasoning we can see what happens in John's Gospel. There the element of the future coming of the Son has disappeared, and there is, already present, thanks to the belief opened up by Jesus, access to life without end, and at the same time a promise of a resurrection on the last day (John 6:54). I do not see why this promise of resurrection on the last day has to be an addition by a different redactor in order to reintroduce the eschatological element which John of himself would have omitted.[5] Rather it seems to me to be totally coherent with what we have seen of the way in which the subversion from within of the apocalyptic imagination by Jesus' eschatological imagination developed, that the time after Jesus be, in fact, the time in which those who are called to Jesus by the Father have access to eternal life and construct a counter-history whose fullness will be revealed and crowned on the last day. Please notice that this last day is no longer the Day which we have seen in the apocalyptic imagination, a day of fulminating vengeance. Rather the last day is a new reality, inconceivable both for the apocalyptic imagination and for the paganism of the eternal return: the end of the human story, not produced by a divine intervention but by the winding down and the tendency toward dissolution that is proper to human time abandoned to itself. That is to say, any historical "apocalypse" will be purely human, and the responsibility for it purely our own.

With this I'm already jumping a little to things which we will see in the next chapter, but it seems to me to be important to do for "the end" something of what we did for "the wrath": that is, show the inner dynamic in the apostolic witness by which the internal coherence of what Jesus had understood before his resurrection came to possess his disciples. Now I would like to pause briefly for a look at a point of method which seems to be important.

The "Canon within the Canon" and "The Church as Interpreter of Scripture"

This is the issue: you will have become aware as we have advanced that some passages of the apostolic witness come to be relativized with respect to others. For example, the apocalyptic passages of Paul in Thessalonians are read in the light of 2 Peter, and I say: well, it was toward the understanding which we find in 2 Peter that the thought of the apostolic group was developing. In this way I manage to say, effectively, that Paul was mistaken in his early expression

---

5. Cf. the opinion of R. Bultmann, one of the great fathers of modern critical theology.

of his understanding of the end, or at least that that understanding was insufficiently worked out, and that little by little he was able to interpret the same data in a different way, in the degree to which he worked out all the consequences of his own discovery of the relationship between the risen victim and God, that is to say, of the experience on the road to Damascus.

Traditionally, when some passages among the texts of the apostolic witness are relativized with respect to others, this is referred to as the search for a "canon within the canon," an expression which was born, I think, to describe the way in which Luther wanted to alter the New Testament so that the centrality of his own doctrine of justification by faith would stand out more. He wanted, for example, to suppress the epistle of James, because it insists that faith without works is dead. More recently those who have criticized Luke and Acts for their clear hints of *Frühkatholizismus* have proceeded along the same principle. The Catholic Church has insisted, over against this tendency, in maintaining the totality of the books (let us remember that the list, or canon, was defined for the first time as recently as the Council of Trent in the sixteenth century), and has promulgated the teaching that, since the sacred texts are the books of the Church, the Church is the sole authentic interpreter of these texts.

There is a way of understanding this business of the Church as the interpreter of the texts as though it meant that, well, there are the texts, and the interpretation is the one which the Magisterium gives, nourished by a panoply of readings taken from the Fathers of the Church and so on. That is, the question of the Church as interpreter of Holy Scripture is understood essentially to be a question of authority, and one is for or against, as the case may be. But, it seems to me that there is a much more profound and important sense in which we must insist on the Church as the interpreter of Scripture, as against all attempts to find an extra-ecclesial point of access to interpret the sacred texts, and it is the sense which I hope to have demonstrated implicitly. It is that the Church is interpreter of the sacred texts insofar as it is the nexus toward which those texts flow. Another way of saying this is to say that, if there is no inner coherence between the reading of the texts and the coming into being of the Church, then there is no access to the inner dynamic of the texts: they are simply ancient texts which may give us sparks of interest and fragments of meaning, but are in no way the foundational texts for every attempt to give meaning to our life.

I say this because it might be protested against the method which

I have used to show the process of the reception of Jesus' eschatological imagination that it is just another attempt to find a canon within the canon and serves to justify any modern idea that one wants to read into the text, where in fact Paul's words about the End, or the Wrath of God, must be read just so, and are just as valid as those of 2 Peter about the end, or of John about love: equally valid, but just different. What I would like to suggest is that it is not just to read my interpretation as the search for a canon within the canon, for I am not attempting to remove or to disqualify any of the texts which there are in the canon. I am trying to show that, reading the texts in this way, even the apparent contradictions which can be seen give witness to the process which brought the Church into existence; and I understand that this process places the apostolic witness as the critical basis which both shows what the Church is and suggests something of the ways in which our living out of our ecclesial life always runs the risk of being unfaithful to what Jesus wanted to bring about.[6]

After this aside, let us move on to my last point in the present chapter, to what I have called "the time of Abel."

The Time of Abel, or the Inhabitability of Time

I would like to take a look at something which is a consequence of what I have been setting out for you, and which I think to be a useful tool in the search which we make as Catholics for an understanding of something of the modern world in which we live and in which we forge our Christian life and preaching.

Let us imagine Cain, sentenced to wander forever over the face of the earth, unable to find a lasting home, always with fear of some vengeance for his brother's murder, and only half-protected by the laws which God gave after that incident, laws whose purpose was to contain the violence of reciprocal vengeance. Cain is getting on now and feels that death draws close. Wherever he goes he hears rumors that something terrible will happen, some fearful end will befall him, with a judgment in which he will be declared guilty. The truth is that that matter of his brother has been clouded from his memory, or is there as a very distant, vague sense of unease. What he knows is that

---

6. Cf. *Dei Verbum* 10b: "The office of interpreting authentically the word of God, oral or written, has been commended only to the Magisterium of the Church, which exercises it in the name of Jesus Christ. However the Magisterium is not above the word of God, but at its service, only teaching that which has been transmitted...."

he has been wandering all over the face of the earth since a certain time ago, without managing to settle anywhere, and it hasn't been for want of trying. He has had to fight bloody wars to protect himself; he has helped others to build sacred frontiers to protect themselves, also, against the violence which spreads everywhere. He spread a theology, he too, in which God is worshipped by people upholding strict laws separating good from bad, pure from impure, so as to keep God safely in place as the guarantor of social order. But now he feels, he knows not how, that things are winding down, coming to such a cosmic end that neither he nor anyone has a real protection against the threat.

Let us imagine him in a hut, not very well built, trying to sleep. Sleep does not come to him easily, because he has a presage of danger, and at times he stays half awake through the night. This night is no different, but suddenly he is fully awake when he realizes that someone has entered, burrowing a small hole in the wall. Cain is frightened: it will be either a thief or a murderer. The intruder seems unalarmed by having been detected, and this is probably because he is young and strong and would have no difficulty in overcoming the old man who is before him, an old man who would once have known how to put such an intruder to the sword. Not only does he not seem alarmed, but he draws close to the one who has intuited him in the darkness, so confirming all the old man's fears that, at last, he will perish defenseless, as he has made so many others to perish.

However, the young man, on whose face can be glimpsed, even in the shadows of the first hours of dawn, certain half-healed scars, says to him: "Fear not, it is I, your brother, do you not remember?" He has to help the old man to remember that strong and handsome youth whom Cain adored, and who was his brother; so much did he adore him that he felt prostrated before him, loving him so much that the only way of being like him was to be instead of him, and he killed him, not out of hatred, but out of envy, devastating excess of a love which grasps at being. This process of remembering his brother is not at all pleasant for the old man, since at every awakening to what had really happened, it shakes him to see what it was that had been driving him since then, what strange and fatal mechanisms of love and hatred interlaced; and his whole story of wandering, of searching for shelter, of killing and driving out to protect himself, all stand revealed as unnecessary. At every step his brother allows him to see what had really been going on, and at each step the old man would like to do what his leathern'd legs will no longer allow him to do: to flee before hearing more, so much does he fear the turning inside out of everything he has come to be.

Nevertheless, the young brother doesn't let him off this strange trial, strange, for in this court, the younger brother is victim, attorney, and judge, and the trial is the process of unblaming the one who did not dare to hear an accusation that never comes. Strangely, as his memory takes body, the old man begins to feel less and less the weight of the threatened end, which he had almost heard roaring about his ears. And he is right to lose that feeling, for the end has already come, but not as a threat: it has come as his brother who forgives him. He begins to glimpse that at the end of this trial he may have no physical strength left, but with all the strength of his heart which is unfolding into youth, he wants to kiss his brother before dying, the rest does not matter....

All this will no doubt have been pretty obvious to you, heavily Dostoyevskian tints and all. What I wanted to suggest is that, in this, very exactly, does the Christian faith consist: in the return of Abel as forgiveness for Cain, and the return of Abel not only as a decree of forgiveness for Cain, but as an insistent presence which gives Cain time to recover his story, and, with the years which remain to him, which may only be days, who knows, to begin to construct another story. This he will manage to do in the degree to which, at every step of that painful process of calling to mind, he manages to stand loose from what he was doing, driven on by his poorly hidden flight in shame, and to build another story in which he has ceased to swing between playing the rôle of hero, who has to face up to a senseless life, or that of the victim, against whom all whisper, and who must protect himself against them all; to build a story that is "other," somewhere between forgotten and unimagined, the story of the brokenhearted fratricide to whom his brother has come back in peace, naked of threat. However the story is to finish, between this arrival of his brother like a thief in the night and the end of his days, Cain will be hard at work in the construction of the story of one who can look into his brother's eyes neither with pride nor with shame. He will look instead with the gratitude of a man who has received himself back at the hands of the one he himself killed, killed to fill the vacuum of the feeling that, before that other, he, Cain, had no "himself" to give, no "himself" with whom to love.

This is the story of which we are talking when we speak of the human story in its working out starting from the resurrection. It is what I call the time of Abel. The time in which the innocent victim is made present to us as forgiveness, and thus, little by little, allows us to let go of all the sacred mechanisms of which we lay hold to fortify ourselves against our own truth. Of course, this process of letting go is violent, because we don't let go easily, or at once. The problem is that, at every step of our removing the sacred, the desacralized element gets resacralized, but under a different form, opposed to the previous sacralization, and we think that, at last, we have managed to set ourselves free from the sacred.

You can multiply examples of this from your experience or your knowledge of history. Let us go no further than the two most powerful enemy twins of this century, whose dregs we all drink to some extent. National Socialism was the fantastic attempt by a prostrated and humiliated nation to create a pure, Aryan sacred, rejecting the whole of that repulsive Jewish and Christian history which seeks to look with compassion on the victim, an attempt so powerful that it created, with full knowledge aforethought, an unimaginable quantity of victims. At the same time as this sacralization there was the great attempt at a definitive desacralization following the thought of Marx: the attempt to get rid, at last, of the deceptive world of religion by building a planned, rational society, without religion, whence all religion was expelled, with a violence no less atrocious. We know now something of how many victims that system had to sacrifice, thinking itself free from religion, and in fact returning to religion's most primitive form: the construction of equality, peace, and social order on the basis of the expulsion of the contaminating element, the bourgeois, the kulak, the small landholder, the priest, the dissident, the suspected dissident, the potential dissident, whoever might doubt the unanimity against the expelled one.

It is not, as some say, that extremes meet, but that the underlying phenomenon is identical. Exactly the same phenomenon can be seen since Christianity desacralized the Roman empire, then going on to sacralize it again, until that project was itself desacralized at the time of the Reformation, and with it the Church, at the same time as the nation-state began to be sacralized, and so on. The strangest thing is not this reality of wars and rumors of wars and revolutions spreading all over the earth, but that it is precisely in the midst of all this that little by little there emerges a disbelief in all of that: the creation of a non-sacred space in terms of ordinary time and ordinary life, where many have a relative peace and distance from all the surrounding disturbances. Here too the same mechanism plays its rôle: when the empire is desacralized, the Church is sacralized in its stead;

when the Church is desacralized, the conscience is sacralized, and so on. However, not all has been a series of swings of the pendulum, but effectively we have become distanced from certain things. It is difficult for someone in "the West" to believe any longer in the evil attributed to witches; the belief that the Jews were responsible for outbreaks of the plague in the Middle Ages lasted for centuries; the attempt to make believe that they were responsible for the ills of society, and so to found a Reich which would last a thousand years, lasted no longer than twelve.

The problem is this: since this series of swings of the pendulum began, that is, since the humble security which was afforded us by a belief in the guilt of the victim began to wither away, there have been no purely good or evil people. Almost nobody escapes from some or other involvement in some degree of what is later considered to be an evil, and this is because that apparently contradictory movement of desacralization and resacralization is at its simultaneous work in the lives of each of us. Consider how this is lived now: in our Western societies those who are called "of the right" tend to sacralize those things which have to do with personal morality: the family, abortion, and so on. At the same time they have a highly secular and secularizing attitude toward social morality, especially in its economic dimension: it should not be controlled, free frontiers, "get the government off our back," end the religious superstition of the past that competition, that is, rivalry at the heart of the group, produces social evils. What is strange of course is that the sacred personal and family morality is strictly dependent on economic and social life, and the attempt to sacralize the former while secularizing the latter produces and exacerbates the world of contradictory desires which form us. This besides, of course, the necessary sequel to every sacralization: the disqualifying of people who do not fit within the scheme, the creation of new impure and profane people.

The contrary position is identical: that which gets called "of the left" tends to be rather more secular in its attitude to personal morality, at the same time as it has sought, at least up until now, to sacralize the social and economic order, building strong frontiers (both physical and ideological), attempting to block desire, to destroy competition and rivalry, with the result, as could be expected, that, on the occasions when it has taken power it has proceeded, a very short time after its installation, to a forced control of personal and matrimonial life and so on. Think of the splendid word which the Cuban revolution coined for this: *La parametración* — fitting your personal life within the acceptable parameters! And woe to them that cannot or will not....

None of us escapes from living in the midst of all these contradictory and oscillating desires and tendencies, and we are all formed from within by means of them. This is the time of Abel, the time of the scandal revealed, where there is no longer any formula for reunion, where there is no easy peace, and in the midst of which the one who refuses to participate in the current game runs the risk of being lynched, but also has to take great care that her way of playing the game is not to seek to be lynched, to sacralize herself as a victim. This is one of the possibilities that only the scandal of the cross has made viable.

The task is to live in the midst of this, learning not to be scandalized either by oneself or by the process, nor by finding oneself living out simultaneous contradictions. Being scandalized means, in the first place, always being in flight from one form of the sacred to another, in a series of strokes of the pendulum where the most that we manage to hide from ourselves is the identity of what is apparently different. The only one who can cease fleeing from these strokes is the Cain who accepts forgiveness, accepts that he has no city, and that there is no need to seek to found it, because the Son of man has no place, like Cain, and his story is built wherever, and has no abiding city, because the new Jerusalem is coming down from heaven.

When Jesus says, "And blessed is whosoever is not scandalized by me" (Matt. 11:6) and Paul preaches the *scandal* of the cross (1 Cor. 1:23), they are revealing, and making habitable, life in the time of Abel. Whoever is not scandalized by Abel, who does not have to flee in scandal from the sacred to the secular and back again to the sacred, without ever leaving that same cyclical movement, is being enabled to accept the contradictions which move him or her and, in the midst of them, to stretch out a hand to the victims of the scandalized sacred in which that person has, him or herself, participated, and to some degree participates still. The peace which Christ gave and which the world does not give, the creation of habitable time, is this peace of Cain in the time of Abel, in patient and humble hoping for the coming of a new heaven and a new earth.

In the next chapter, before focusing on what would seem to be the theme which follows on naturally from this, that is, on the nature of hope, at which we will look in our penultimate chapter, we are going to examine the passages of the Gospels called (wrongly in my view) "apocalyptic," to see if those texts are "at home" in the midst of the eschatological perception which I am attempting to set forth.

Training the Eyes on the Coming

In our previous chapter we began to fathom what I described as the subversion from within of the apocalyptic imagination by the coming into being of the eschatological imagination. This latter imagination is nothing other than Jesus' mind fixed on the utterly effervescent goodness and vivaciousness of God. I wanted to show you how the same process of shearing the violence from the human perception of God, which we have seen applied to other dimensions of that perception, also applies to the slow process by which there came about that quality of time which I have called "of Abel," but which we might also call the time of the Church. This is the inhabitable time in which we humans learn how not to be scandalized, fleeing from sacred refuge to sacred refuge, thinking that, now at last, we are free, but instead beginning patiently to construct a new universality around the victim.

In this chapter an analysis of the treatment of matters eschatological in each of the Gospels will occupy us, so that we may see how the process of subversion from within of the apocalyptic imagination was already at work very early on among the apostolic group in the light of the Lord's resurrection. Let us begin within the end, with the most obvious version of the process, so as then to examine, with better fruit, the older texts.

John: The Judgment Already Realized

In John's Gospel there is no eschatological discourse as such, comparable to those we will examine from the synoptic Gospels. Instead there is an extended meditation about judgment which weaves through the whole Gospel. As we saw when we looked at the way he set out the coming of the Holy Spirit, John tends to give us a series of apparently contradictory phrases, which rub together, often in an ironic way, until we grasp the point of what he's saying. He uses the same method when he explains the judgment. Let us turn to it:

When Jesus speaks with Nicodemus, he says to him:

> For God so loved the world that he gave his only begotten Son, that whosoever believeth in him should not perish, but have everlasting life. For God sent not his Son into the world to judge the world, but that the world through him might be saved. He that believeth on him is not judged; but he that believeth not is judged already, because he has not believed in the name of the only begotten Son of God. The judgment consists in this: that light is come into the world and men loved darkness rather than light, because their deeds were evil. For every one that doeth evil hateth the light, neither cometh to the light, lest his deeds should be reproved. But he that doeth truth cometh to the light, that his deeds may be made manifest, that they are wrought in God. (John 3:16–21)

John's presuppositions are by now familiar to us. God does not want to judge anybody. The coming of the Son into the world has as its end to create a belief in the absolute aliveness of God and to empower us in this way to act as if death were not, thus being set free from our compulsion to act out in a way governed by the kingdom of death. The one who believes that Jesus was in fact sent by God and is the authentic witness of God's utter vivaciousness which knows not death, that one already, by this fact, begins to be able to be unbound from his or her previous way of acting and begins to live according to the light. People like this do not fear the exposing of their previous participation in the system or mechanism of the dominion of death, because that is being left behind as they begin to allow themselves to be transformed into a mansion of life without end in the midst of the world. Such people will not be judged, for they have left the world which judges, condemns, and casts out, in order to begin to live according to God who neither judges, nor condemns, nor casts out. Those, however, who do not accept the light, who do not want their complicity in the order of death to stand revealed, preferring the shelter of the old and murderous lie, such are indeed judged, for they have remained entirely within the system which judges, condemns, and casts out. For people like this, the light is a threat to be detested, as the police battalion detests the officer who gives witness that all were involved in conspiring to fabricate evidence against a supposed delinquent, or the colleagues behind the tills in the bank hate their fellow cashier who reveals the little tricks by which all were quietly augmenting their meager salaries.... Such dissidents must go.

The verses which I have just quoted say clearly that God did not send his Son into the world to judge the world. However a little later the concept gets developed further, and in an apparently contradictory way. Jesus has just cured the infirm man at the pool of Bethesda and is talking to those who were infuriated by his action:

> For as the Father raiseth up the dead and quickeneth them; even so the Son quickeneth whom he will. For the Father judgeth no man, but hath committed all judgment unto the Son: that all men should honor the Son, even as they honor the Father.... Verily, verily I say unto you, he that heareth my word and believeth on him that sent me, hath everlasting life, and shall not come unto judgment, but is passed from death unto life.... For as the Father hath life in himself; so hath he given to the Son to have life in himself; and hath given him authority to execute judgment also, because he is the Son of man...I can of my own self do nothing: as I hear, I judge: and my judgment is just; because I seek not my own will, but the will of the Father which hath sent me.[1]

Do you notice the change? Earlier it was said that the Father did not send his Son to judge the world, but this now receives a nuance: the Father judges nobody, but has handed to the Son, precisely as Son of man, all authority to judge. The Son's authority to judge comes because he is, like his Father, full and effervescent life. But this Son of man quite without any shading into death does not judge on his own account, but as he hears his Father speak, and it is for this that his judgment is just.

Does not this seem contradictory? On the one hand it says that the Father judges nobody, but the Son does; then it seems that the Son exercises this judgment (and let us remember that the Father did not send him to judge the world), but not according to his own criteria, but according to what he hears from the Father (who, let us remember, judges no one). All this is part of the process of bathing the language of judgment in irony or, said in other words, the pro-

---

1. John 5:21–22, 24, 26–27, 30 The archaic form "to quicken" captures rather better than modern equivalents the force of the vivacity and effervescence of God of which I have been talking.

cess of the subversion from within of the concept of judgment. The Father, in fact, does not judge, but the Son, absolute witness to the life and effervescence of the Father, comes to be Judge in the measure in which he obeys his Father. What he does in obeying his Father is to reveal the murderous lie of the world, and it is *as victim of that murderous lie that he becomes the Judge.* That is, Jesus did not come to judge, but, insofar as people reject him, he, as the victim who reveals the dominion of death and is the criterion by which its mechanism is understood, comes to be its judge.

Let me give a comparison to make the matter clearer: we can imagine a perturbed society, perhaps threatened by an outside enemy, but where even so there are strong divisions. Suddenly, very serious accusations are raised against someone, of being a spy or something equivalent. It would be convenient that this person were in some way liminal, that is, half in and half out of that society. This threshold has traditionally been occupied by Jews in European society, but with a change of place and circumstance it could be any other liminal person, a half-caste in a land of white people, and so on. We can imagine that the evidence against this person is not very convincing, nor is it really clear what motive this person might have for spying for the enemy. However, what is lacking in weight of evidence is compensated for by the hatred evoked by the half-insider, half-outsider status of the accused. These factors make it much more probable that the accused be "guilty," even with no evidence to back this up. Well, the person is tried and, of course, is found guilty, and is led to prison or before a firing squad.

Thus far all is normal. We have an accused and a lynch mob; placed between them we have a judge and a jury who give legal cover to what the mob wants. The rôles of judge and accused are well-defined. However, just imagine that a few years later, while the accused is in prison, or six feet under, evidence begins to emerge which suggests that all that had gone before was orchestrated by the forces at work in the society of the period. Orchestrated, I say, not in the simple sense that someone forged evidence (which they may have, of course), but orchestrated blindly in the sense that all were involved in demanding sentence against the accused, and where the issue of evidence was only a light part of the matter. All this begins to come out, and there is a glimmer of perception of what had really been happening, a glimmer that the participants were unable to perceive at the time of the trial. It will not be long before a journalist or a historian draws the obvious conclusion: in what seemed to be a judgment of the society against an infractor, it was in fact the society which was being judged. In the long run the victim of that trial, being innocent, comes to be the criterion by which the hypocrisy, dirt, and mendacity of the society in question is judged. That is, the victim is judge *as victim*. By being the innocent victim, that person becomes the criterion, the principle of judgment, of the lynching society. The whole society of the era is under judgment for its blind participation in that lynching.

You can doubtless imagine just such historical incidents from your own countries or areas of interest. As I was describing the process, I took as underlying model the trial of Alfred Dreyfus, a Jewish officer in the French army toward the end of the last century. However, even though it is beyond reasonable doubt that French society is especially reprehensible under every possible aspect of this case, the trial against the writer Oscar Wilde in England shows that even in that small Nordic island similar things do just get to happen. What I am claiming is that very few people, today, understand those trials *except from the point of view of the victim*. That is, all understand that it was the judging society that was, in fact, judged by reason of its action against the victim. Our problem must be learning not to say, "If I had been there, I would have had no part in that lynch, when our forebears killed the prophets..." but to wonder about the ways, hidden to us, in which we *are* participating in exactly those same mechanisms, after the manner of the blindness of our forebears.

All this is to bring out the way in which John speaks of judgment. The Father judges no one, and neither does Jesus; but Jesus, as victim of the murderous mechanisms of society, has come to be the criterion, the judging point, for it to be seen how we humans are behaving. Those who have begun to shed the murderous blindness, beginning to live as if death were not, and because of that, being free of the lies by which society builds its frontiers, they have passed through judgment. That is, the victim as judge does not judge them *because they have not judged*. They have not participated in the judgment which casts out. Those who do participate remain under judgment, not because either the Father or Jesus seek to judge them, but because by their own behavior they have remained on the timorous side of judgment and refuse to come out into the light so that the truth of their acting out may stand revealed.

In this way we can understand the development of the argument in John. In chapter 8, after declaring himself the light of the world, Jesus says to the Pharisees:

> Ye judge according to the flesh; I judge no one. And yet even if I were to judge, my judgment is true, because I am not alone, but I and the Father who sent me. (John 8:15–17)

Do you see the subversion from within of the notion of judgment? To judge according to the flesh is exactly to judge from within the scheme of the murderous lie. And Jesus does not judge, except in the sense in which, by means of his vindication by the Father, he, the victim, has come to be the true criterion by which judgment is given. He is, so to speak, a passive judge.

We see the same thing in John 12, when Jesus announces that his "hour" has come:

> Now is the judgment of this world: now shall the prince of this world be cast out, and I, when I am lifted up from the earth will draw all people to me. (John 12:31–32)

The judgment is carried out against the order of this world, founded on the murderous lie, and this judgment has as its centerpiece Jesus "lifted up from the earth." That is, when Jesus is cast out, he is in fact constituted judge of every system of casting out, which, from that moment begins to wither away. Once again we see that, from the cross of Jesus, the victim is judge *as* victim. It is this also that is promised with the coming of the Holy Spirit in John 16:

> When he comes, he will convict the world with respect to sin, to what justice [or goodness] consists in, and with respect to judgment: with respect to sin, because they did not believe in me; with respect to justice, because I am going to my Father, and you shall see me no more, and with respect to judgment, because the prince of this world has been judged.
>
> (John 16:8–11)

That is to say that the defense attorney will have the rôle which we have seen, of subverting the understanding of sin from within, by means of Jesus' expulsion, his going to the Father. Sin is now to be understood starting from the refusal to live outside the parameters of the murderous lie, the possibility of which living was opened up by Jesus. Goodness, or justice, will be understood from Jesus' going to his Father: it is our flexible imitation of this which will constitute goodness; the judgment is the revelation of the mechanism of this world, whose power is emptied out as it is revealed by the innocent victim.

Thus far the way in which John works the theme of judgment, subverting it from within by the light of the criterion provided by the expelled victim. There are a few more points in the Johannine treatment of matters eschatological that are worth considering before moving on to the synoptic Gospels. John is not on the way to developing a merely existential eschatology, but is aware that this vision of his is related to living in history. So he introduces a principle of judgment in history which applies to both the living and the dead. That is, there will be a final judgment where will stand revealed the whole historical way in which the dynamic which Jesus has introduced into the world has been lived out by us. There is a clear understanding that Jesus' subversive judgment will be apparent on the last day, and will be the criterion in whose light the living and the dead are judged. We have already seen the passage from John 5 where Jesus says that whoever hears his word and believes in the one who sent him *already* possesses eternal life, and will not be called to judgment. Now look at what follows, part of which I left out for clarity's sake when I last quoted it:

> Verily, verily, I say unto you, the hour is coming, and now is, when the dead shall hear the voice of the Son of God: and hearing, they shall live. For, as the Father hath life in himself; so hath he given to the Son to have life in himself; and hath given him authority to execute judgment also, because he is the Son of man. Marvel not at this: for the hour is coming, in which all that are in the graves shall hear his voice, and shall come forth; they that have done good, unto the resurrection of life; and they that have done evil, unto the resurrection of judgment.
>
> (John 5:25–29)

Here it can clearly be seen that God, who is absolutely alive, and thus knows neither death nor human temporality, has conceded to the Son to be judge of the quick and the dead, extending to all humans of all generations the same criteria which we have seen Jesus to have introduced into the world. The final judgment will be a judgment in reverse in which the whole of human history will be illuminated by the criterion of the victim, who is judge *as* victim. Now let us turn to the way in which Mark bears witness to the subversion of the apocalyptic by the eschatological.

Mark: The Subtlety of the Hour[2]

Mark 13 is probably the earliest among the eschatological discourses we have in the synoptic Gospels, and it begins, significantly, with the prophecy of the destruction of the Temple. Shortly afterward, Peter, James, John, and Andrew ask Jesus:

> Tell us, when shall these things be? and what shall be the sign when all these things shall be brought to an end? (Mark 13:4)

Please notice that the link between the prophecy of the destruction of the Temple and the end of everything is made not by Jesus but by the disciples, and immediately afterward we have one of Jesus' famous non-replies. He does not answer their question directly but begins to give instructions for how to live in the period which is to be inaugurated by his death. And his instructions are negative rather than positive.

In the first place, pay no attention to people who come as Messiah, or some sort of savior, leading many people astray. Jesus gives to understand that his own coming will *not* be of this sort. As we shall see later, his coming will be absolutely manifest, but not with that sort of manifestation. Secondly, do not be alarmed by the wars, battles, and portents which are to come. That is to say, not only should they not pay attention to the possible theological value of the prophets who come, but they must also learn to distance themselves from attributing theological importance to the violent events of this world. They have no such importance. Of course, these things are going to happen, and Jesus knows very well that, precisely because he has invalidated the easy formula for making peace, there will be wars and nations will rise up against nations: these are the first pains of what has been produced by him. They are, so to speak, the negative counterpart of what he has inaugurated, this continuous process which we have seen in the time of Abel, the flight from false sacralization to false sacralization, without ever leaving reciprocal violence.

In the midst of all this, the disciple must walk with care, for he cannot associate himself with this process. Rather, this is a description of the reality in whose midst the disciple must give witness to his following of Jesus, of his belief in another kingdom, distinct from the kingdoms which seek to found themselves on reciprocal violence.

---

2. It is recommended that the reader have Mark 13 open to accompany this section.

In the midst of this process the disciple will always be an outsider, and always a potential victim, potential traitor, potential subversive, and so on. In the midst of all this conflictual reality, the good news about God and the coming into existence of the arduously constructed kingdom of universality, which we have already seen, will be borne slowly and almost silently to all nations.

It seems to me very significant that it be in this context that Jesus warns against being worried in advance about what to say before the tribunals. In a world ruled by the lynch mechanism, a typical attitude which will come about will be that of those who consider themselves victims and for that reason are always preparing themselves against accusations. Which of us has not fantasized a trial in the midst of accusations which we manage to rebut by the power of our argument? Isn't this one of the ways of proving our worth? An extraordinary and triumphant self-justification? Well, Jesus prohibits us this fantasy. The Holy Spirit, the defense counsellor, is the one who will defend us, so that it is in the degree to which we cease to worry about defending ourselves, which is the same as saying, cease to worry about justifying ourselves, that the defending Spirit will declare innocent the victims. Let us be clear that this is not a guarantee that we're going to get off unharmed from the trials and "legal" lynchings of the world, for many have indeed perished under just such circumstances, most notably Jesus. However, in the long run, the innocence of the victim will be established. Another way of saying this: if we are preoccupied about our defense, then we are still prisoners of the violence of the world. Our paranoia, our anxiousness to defend and to justify ourselves is nothing other than that. Jesus tells us that the Defense Counsellor gives us such freedom that we do not even have to justify or defend ourselves and that this trial, this process, of those who are learning to live free in the midst of the persecuting turbulences of this world, is what discipleship looks like in the time that is installed by his death.

It is in this context of the collapse of all the normal forms of building human unity, including that within the family, where children, parents and siblings hate each other, that the patient universality of the kingdom which does not cast out is to be built.

Jesus then moves on to a description of something which in all probability refers to the fall of Jerusalem, to judge by the references to Judaea: that fall will be a terrible reality, as indeed it was. But not even that, for all its horror, is to be read in a theological key. All of that has nothing to do with the coming of the Messiah, and the disciple must learn not to read that fall in theological terms, not to pay attention to supposed signs and prodigies which will so give the impression of coming from God that even the elect will run the risk of being lead astray by them.

After having laid the foundations about that to which one must *not* pay attention, Jesus turns to describing his coming. In the first place he uses apocalyptic language, taken from the book of Daniel: the sun will be darkened, the moon will give forth no light, and so on. Please notice that this way of talking does *not* indicate some supposed divine intervention shaking up these heavenly bodies. The language depends on the Semitic vision of earth and sky as a single reality where the stars, the sun, and the moon were hung in the vault of heaven. What is being described is the way in which *earthly,* that is to say, human violence, shakes all of creation. We are speaking once again of human violence, a social and cultural upheaval of ever greater magnitude. It is in the midst of a human violence which shakes the foundations of all creation that the Son of man will be seen on the clouds, in strength and majesty. That vision of the Son of man, as we have already seen, comes from Daniel, and the clouds will be appearing again shortly. It is starting from this appearance of the Son of man that the angels will come out to gather together the chosen ones from every corner of the earth.

After this Jesus speaks to the disciples about the fig tree. You will remember that, not long before, he had cursed the fig tree which was barren, even though it was not the season for figs (Mark 11:12–14). The fig tree symbolizes both Israel and the Temple, and Jesus is bringing about a new fig tree, which will produce fruit, and it is in the degree to which this new fig tree produces fruit in the midst of the circumstances which Jesus has just described that the disciples will start to understand that the coming of the Son of man is at the door. And all this will happen in this generation, the generation which begins with Jesus' death and which will begin to live the fruits of the uncovering of the innocence of the victim. Jesus is quite clear: heaven and earth will pass away, but his words will not pass away. That is to say, the teaching which he has come to bring, leaving open and exposed the mechanism of the randomly chosen victim will be, from now on, the inexorable, though hidden, dynamic of history, and it is in its light that everything will be reconceptualized — which has in fact happened. Once said, what Jesus said can never be totally hidden again, and any attempt to do so (like, for example, the Nazi attempt) fatally fails in the long run.

At the end of his discourse, Jesus returns to the initial question of his disciples, so as to refuse them an answer to their question "when?" It is not a matter of a "when"; it's about how always to be alive to the presence of the victim. It is a question of the basic attitude of the disciple in the time inaugurated by Jesus' death: always to have the capacity for a flexibility of vision in order to recognize the victim, wherever that victim be and under whatever form that victim appear, so as to know how to go out to meet that victim. The whole of the time between the death of Jesus and the end of history gyrates around this dynamic of having sight made flexible by knowing how to receive the victim.

After this there follows one of the most brilliant passages in Mark, which in a certain sense gives the key for reading all that has gone before. The master goes off, handing out tasks and demanding that the servants remain alert:

> Watch ye therefore: for ye know not when the master of the house cometh, at evening, or at midnight, or at cockcrow, or in the morning: lest coming suddenly he find you sleeping.
> (Mark 13:35–36)

With this we understand something fundamental about Mark: that he writes in a self-referential way. For this passage, the last before the beginning of the Passion, refers exactly to the events of the Passion which are to unfold. The coming of the master will take place *in the handing over of Jesus,* for it is at evening that he hands himself over to the disciples in the form of the Eucharist, at midnight that he is handed over by Judas, who comes when the disciples are asleep; at cockcrow he is betrayed (handed over) by Peter, and at dawn he is handed over by the high priest to the Romans for execution. Just in case we have not understood this, Jesus repeats before the high priest the phrase about the coming of the Son of man on the clouds, telling him that he will himself see this phenomenon:

> ...and ye shall see the Son of man sitting on the right hand of power and coming in the clouds of heaven. (Mark 14:62)

Then, in the scene of the crucifixion, even though it was midday, the whole sky was darkened (the raised Son of man coming on clouds), and immediately after Jesus expires, that is, hands over his Spirit, there begins the process of the angels who seek out the chosen ones from the four winds, for it is a Roman centurion who says:

Truly this man was the Son of God. (Mark 15:39b)

I hope that you see some of the threads of subtlety which are to be found beneath Mark's text. The so-called apocalyptic discourse of Jesus is nothing other than a brilliant exercise in the subverting from within of the apocalyptic imagination. It has as its end to teach the disciples how to live in the times that are to come, the time which I called "of Abel." Above all it seeks to train the disciples with respect to what must be their deepest eschatological attitude: the absolutely flexible state of alert in order to perceive the coming of the Son of man, the one who is seated at the right hand of God, in the most hidden and subtle forms in which, in fact, he comes. That is, we are dealing with instructions about how to live with the mind fixed on the things that are above, where Christ is seated with God: not glued to some fantasy, but learning to perceive the comings of the Son of man in the acts of betrayal, of rejection, of handing over, and of lynching. We can compare this with the experience of Elijah on Mount Horeb, who had to learn that God was not in the tempest, nor in the earthquake, nor in the fire, but in the still, small voice which passes by unperceived (1 Kings 19:11–13). We're dealing with a similar experience: Jesus was explaining to the disciples that the state of alert in the face of his coming is a training in the perception, not of that which is bruited abroad, nor of what glistens appealingly, but of the way that all the majesty and splendor of God is to be found in the almost imperceptible victim, on the way out of being.

Thus far Mark, to give us the tone of our reading. We are going to see that Luke and Matthew, each in a different way, take some elements of this vision, adding, sharpening, and emphasizing particular perceptions of their own. Since a large part of Mark 13 is also present in those Gospels, I am not going to repeat the reading of the entire text, but in each case will underscore some of the points they develop and emphasize.

Luke: The Coming as Revelation

We have already seen, when we looked at the simultaneous coming about of the possibility of universality and of the new quality of time, that Luke makes explicit a separation between the prophecy of Jesus applied to the Temple of Jerusalem and life in the "time of the nations," which would also be the time of the Church. We have seen the inner dynamic which led to this separation. Here I would like to point out that this separation has another effect, with respect to the comings of the Son of man. We saw, in Mark, that, owing to the self-referential nature of the text, what we have is an indication of the coming of the Son which occurs principally at his crucifixion: this is the coming of the Son, and it ushers in a period of time during which our living is to be fixed on just such "comings" in our own lives. Luke takes care to distinguish the comings. He does not remove the coming on the cross, which is for him the central watershed of history and opens the time of the nations, but he does begin to give clearer signs of a final coming in glory at the end of history, which is to be public and notorious, as a distinct happening. And this coming takes the form of the revelation, the disclosing, of the Son of man.

Let us read, for example, this passage:

The days will come when ye shall desire to see one of the days of the Son of man, and ye shall not see it. And they shall say to you, See here; or, see there: go not after them, nor follow them. For like lightning, that flashes out of one end of heaven to the other, so shall also the Son of man be in his day. But first must he suffer many things and be rejected of this generation.

(Luke 17:22–25)

Here we see how Jesus explains that the victim, risen and seated at the right hand of God, will have his day: it will not be necessary to look for him in a special way, because the moment will come in which the risen victim will be the principle which illuminates all of human history and reality. And this illumination will be absolutely evident and will happen in the midst of the most apparently normal life: the people surrounding Noah and Lot were just carrying on their entirely normal lives when, of a sudden, judgment came:

Even thus shall it be on the day when the Son of man is revealed. (Luke 17:30)

We begin to understand that Jesus is talking about his final coming in glory as a brilliant revelation of what has really been going on throughout the whole of normal time and life. And the revelation will be the revelation from the new criterion which we have already seen to have been introduced into history, that is, the criterion of the victim. Thus, when Jesus describes to them how absolutely normal will be the time at which all this is going to happen, the disciples ask Jesus *where* this is to be, and Jesus' reply is at the same time humorous and to the heart of the matter:

> Wheresoever the body is, there will the vultures be gathered.
>
> (Luke 17:37)

That is to say, there is no "where"; what there is instead is the criterion of the victim, and that can happen anywhere. The question is: how have I related to the body of the victim? Do I feed on his body and blood while seeking quietly and discreetly to create the universality of the kingdom? Or do I rather participate, maybe without realizing it, in the production of such corpses?

This notion that Jesus came to bring a revelation of what is really going on, a real discrimination of hearts, is a marked emphasis in Luke, who from the outset underlines Jesus' being a sign of contradiction, so that the thoughts of the hearts of many will be laid open (Luke 2:35). He also repeats twice (Luke 8:17; 12:2–3) what Matthew only quotes once (Matt. 10:26–27):

> For there is nothing covered that shall not be revealed; neither hid, that shall not be known.

So the second coming will be a revelation of what has been going on throughout history in the light of the criterion of the risen victim. This we find emphasized once more in the second "apocalyptic discourse" in Luke, the discourse which occupies the same place in his Gospel as it does in Mark's, that is, immediately before the Passion.

Luke emphasizes all the problems and portents which will characterize the generation inaugurated by Jesus' death, with all its perplexities and torments, since the old way to make peace is missing. However, the very development of this time should be a motive for the disciples to take heart:

> And when these things begin to come to pass, then look up, and lift up your heads, for your redemption draweth nigh.
>
> (Luke 21:28)

In the midst of this time of conflict, the fact that all this is happening *is itself the sign* that the innocent victim is arriving and subverting the whole present order. It is in this context that Jesus exhorts the disciples to stay alert:

And take heed to yourselves, lest at any time your hearts be overcharged with surfeiting, and drunkenness, and cares of this life, and so that day come upon you unawares. For as a snare shall it come on all them that dwell on the face of the whole earth. Watch therefore, and pray always that you may have the strength to escape all these things which will come to pass, and to stand before the Son of man. (Luke 21:34–36)

So we are promised an absolutely public and unexpected final coming, which will be patent to all, and in the face of which it is the disciples' task to have so acted in the midst of the tribulations that they are still standing, have managed to persevere in solidarity with the victim, when all is revealed. In this way, just as the Son of man, the risen victim, is standing at the right hand of God, they will also be standing who have lived with their minds fixed on him.

I hope that this is enough to see something of the directions in which Luke develops what was already in Mark, but according to his own interests and emphases. Now let us move on to Matthew.

Matthew: Imagining the Banquet

Our principal evidence in Matthew is in chapters 24 and 25, although there are also many eschatological elements in his parables. I'll begin by pointing to moments where Matthew, although he tells the same story as the other evangelists, adds a slightly different touch. We will take two examples: the parable of the murderous tenants (Matt. 21:33–43) and the parable of the king who gave a wedding banquet for his son (Matt. 22:1–14). If we read Luke's treatment of the same parables (Luke 20:9–19; Luke 14:16–24), there is a very interesting difference in both cases. At the end of Luke's version of the parable of the tenants, Jesus asks:

What therefore shall the lord of the vineyard do unto them [i.e., the tenants]?

and then goes on, *himself,* to answer:

He shall come and destroy these tenants and shall give the vineyard to others. (Luke 20:16)

In Matthew's version, by contrast, Jesus asks the same question:

... what will he do unto those tenants?

but he does not answer. The answer is given by his audience:

> They say unto him: He will miserably destroy those wicked men
> and will let out his vineyard unto others. (Matt. 21:41)

That is, the important thing is how the *listeners* imagine God to be.

If we look at Luke's account of the parable of the wedding banquet which the king organizes for his son, it ends with the king's instruction to oblige all those who are found out there to come in, for none of those originally invited will enter in (Luke 14:23–24). In Matthew the story does not end there, but has an addition:

> And when the king came in to see the guests, he saw there a
> man which had not on a wedding garment: and he saith unto
> him, Friend, how camest thou in hither not having a wedding
> garment? And the man was speechless. Then said the king to
> his servants, Bind him hand and foot and cast him into the outer
> darkness; there shall be weeping and gnashing of teeth.
> (Matt. 22:11–14)

Let us remember that this business of not "wearing a wedding garment" cannot be read as a reference to someone's *moral* behavior, for Matthew has emphasized that all were called in, good and bad alike. Besides, it is known that the custom of that age and place was to provide tunics to place over one's street clothes to participate in a wedding party, and these would have been at the disposal of all the guests on their way in, without the slightest consideration for how good or bad they were.

Here there is something of what we had in the previous parable. The problem with the silent guest is that *he does not imagine himself to be at a wedding banquet*, but in a place of judgment, and for this reason does not dare to speak when he is addressed, and so receives treatment *according to his imagination*. Exactly the same thing happens in the parable of the talents, where Matthew and Luke coincide more exactly. The problem of the servant who received one talent and went and buried it is *not* its lack of yield, but how he imagined that his master would treat him:

> Lord, I knew thee that thou art a hard man, reaping where thou
> hast not sown, and gathering where thou hast not strewed: and

I was afraid, and went and hid thy talent in the earth: lo there thou hast that is thine. (Matt. 25:24–25)

In this case it is Luke who makes the situation more explicit; this, I think, is because the manoeuvre is less common in his Gospel, while for Matthew it is typical of his way of speaking. In Luke the master says:

Out of thine own mouth will I judge thee, thou wicked servant. . . . (Luke 19:22)

And that is exactly what happens. Once again it is the subject's imagination of his master that is absolutely determinant of his behavior. One who imagines his master as free, audacious, generous, and so on, takes risks, and himself enters into a fruitfulness that is ever richer and more effervescently creative; while one whose imagination is bound by the supposed hardness of the master lives in function of that binding of the imagination, and remains tied, hand and foot, in a continuous, and maybe even an eternal, frustration.

This will do as a way into Matthew's way of reading the same "apocalyptic" discourse that we have been looking at in Mark and Luke. I would now like to show how Matthew explains Christian living in the midst of the time inaugurated by Jesus' death, because it includes some tones proper to Matthew which show how he understood the same dynamic of the subversion from within of apocalyptic language. Many of the verses are identical with those of Mark and Luke, but let us concentrate on the different nuances:

For nation shall rise against nation, and kingdom against kingdom: and there shall be famines, and pestilences, and earthquakes in divers places. All these are the beginning of sorrows. Then shall they deliver you up to be afflicted, and shall kill you: and ye shall be hated of all nations for my sake. *And then shall many be scandalized, and shall betray one another, and shall hate one another.* And many false prophets shall rise and shall deceive many. *And because iniquity shall abound, the love of many shall wax cold.* But he that shall resist unto the end shall be saved. (Matt. 24:7–13)

I have highlighted the phrases which are proper to Matthew because they offer us a hint as to how he understands the time which Jesus is ushering in.

Let us notice first Matthew's use of the word "scandal," a term that is especially present in his Gospel. Matthew understands very well that Jesus is in fact a scandal for the order of this world, for there is a special beatitude in his Gospel which we have seen:

> And blessed is whosoever shall not be scandalized at me.
>
> (Matt. 11:6)

That is, the presence of what Jesus has brought about will appear in the eyes of many as the introduction of a perpetual scandal into history, precisely because it will bring about the collapse of all that seemed good, gradually voiding the distinction between goodies and baddies, hindering the way social order has been constructed until now, so that those who follow Jesus will themselves be causes of stumbling, and many will be scandalized by them; either that, or having started to follow Jesus, they will themselves be scandalized on account of the paths into which their discipleship leads them. The result will be the hate and denunciation of those who, as always, want to keep the good good, and the bad bad, people who cannot tolerate the subversion from within which has in fact been introduced by the following of the innocent victim. I already indicated, when I sketched out what I called "the time of Abel," that it is a time of scandal, where people do not have a place of refuge. On account of this the attitude of disciples is that of those who are scandalized neither by themselves, nor by what they live, nor by that to which they are accomplice, the world of secularizations and scandalized attempts to resacralize.

The second point concerns how Matthew understands it as normal that *iniquity shall abound,* that is, increase, and that this is a constant. In fact, from John the Baptist until the death of Jesus, the kingdom of heaven has suffered violence, and the violent take it by storm (Matt. 11:12). With the collapse of the security offered by the Law and the Prophets, there is no longer any way to contain violence, and it will increase. There are no more artificial frontiers thanks to the double-edged sword which Jesus introduced into the human story, and *love shall wax cold.* In fact it is indeed extraordinary that it could even have been perceived that love, the basis of social bonding, should grow cold in the degree to which the forms of social order enter into collapse, bearing us on toward that result, also a two-edged sword, which we all know well: the invention of the "modern individual," apparently without deep bonds of solidarity.

The same process which enabled there to be born an understanding of the sacred dignity of the human person has also brought about a way of being an individual in which the bonds of solidarity and of love are deemed either unnecessary or an active impediment to the development of society. It is in the midst of this process of ambiguity that the disciple lives, the one who is not to be scandalized.

However, the most interesting part of Matthew's treatment of the apocalyptic discourse is not to be found in the discourse itself, but in the great parables which he annexes to that discourse: those of the wise and foolish maidens, of the talents, and of the last judgment. This is Matthew's way of interpreting Jesus' eschatological discourse, his commentary on what he has inherited from Mark and his other sources. Of these parables the first and last have no strict parallel in any other Gospel. We will see that in all three cases we are dealing not with a way of talking about some terrifying future, but about how to live in the here and now.

First the maidens. The fact that they are called wise and foolish takes us back to the end of the Sermon on the Mount, where the wise man builds on the rock and the foolish man on sand (Matt. 7:24–27). Here, however, the emphasis is placed on the way of living during the time when alertness is demanded. The conclusion of the parable is:

Watch therefore, for ye know neither the day nor the hour wherein the Son of man cometh. (Matt. 25:13)

All the maidens slumbered; all were taken by surprise by the arrival of the bridegroom: that is not the problem. The problem lies elsewhere: the foolish ones had not considered how to live during the delay. They imagined a rapid arrival and because of this had not taken the precautions of prudence for the long vigil: they had not filled their vessels. The wise maidens are those who had prepared themselves to sit out the duration. That is, having extra oil and building on the rock are the same thing: the patient, tranquil work that is, furthermore, non-transferable, of structuring a life in vigilant expectation, because no one knows the hour. Thus when the bridegroom comes they are not taken by surprise, for the whole patient structure of their lives has been toward this. The fact that the bridegroom should say to the foolish ones that he knows them not means that it has been their whole life which has not been one of preparation for his coming.

Then comes the parable of the talents, which we have already looked at a little. Once again it is a question of how to live in the here and now: the end is simply a confirmation of an acting out that was fuelled by the way in which each one imagined the master. The one whose mind is fixed on the goodness, creativity, generosity and boldness of the master acts accordingly and sees that imagination confirmed, or rather multiplied to superabundance. The one who works with a mind scandalized by the hardness, complication, and severity of the master sees that imagination confirmed at the end. It is not the end that is interesting, however, but rather the attitude to be cultivated in the here and now.

Finally we have the most grandiose parable of all: that of the sheep and the goats. This is in no way a description of a future gathering beyond the grave. Rather, with all the splendor of apocalyptic language, the time in which we live is being qualified. The criterion for judgment is already present in the midst of the world; we do not have to wait until later. The criterion of judgment is the victim which is the principle of separation just as victim: exactly what we saw in John's Gospel. The final judgment adds *nothing* new to what has been lived out in the here and now. Living in the midst of the world of scandal which we have seen, shaken by the impossibility of maintaining structures, of upholding distinctions, where the efforts to determine who is an insider and who an outsider become hesitant and maybe get much more violent before falling suddenly away: whoever, living in the midst of all this, has known how to stretch out a hand to the precarious, to those who are on their way out of existence, to those deemed scandalous and for that reason excluded, whoever has done that, has done it to Jesus. This was, after all, the rôle of Jesus, the scandalous transgressor who turned out to be the innocent victim: that of introducing into the midst of the human story the possibility that those who are not scandalized might build the universal kingdom.

Whether people have heard of Jesus or not, or whether they have an explicitly religious motivation or not, is not an issue. By entering into the dynamic of those who are not scandalized, which means *because they have paid no heed to the judgment which the world makes* concerning those in prison, the sick, the naked, liminal people of every category, they have already passed through judgment, and it doesn't affect them. Those who, with all their spirituality and their adhesion to an established religion, have accepted the world's judgment on those people, have been scandalized by them, Jesus knows them not. This I understood quite clearly at some point in the crisis produced by AIDS, accustomed as I was to hearing talk of AIDS as a punishment from God or a judgment on such and such a behavior. Along with this attitude went another which suggested that, since these people deserve what has befallen them, it's not worth the bother of doing something to alleviate the problem. And here's the irony of the thing: God's judgment is very real and very terrible, but its working is the inverse of what such people imagine. By separating ourselves from our sisters and brothers in need, alleging reasons of religion to boot, we run grave risk of eternal fire, because God's judgment arrives as the clamor of the neighbor in need. The judge is judge as victim. Whoever attends them confronts no judgment. Those who do not *have already separated themselves into goathood.* I think that AIDS, for example, might be interpreted as a judgment of God, but it works as a question: a catastrophe has occurred; are you prepared to ignore the judgment of this world and stretch a hand toward those who are on their way out of existence? Or are you separating yourself into goathood, thinking yourself a sheep?

You can multiply examples for yourselves from your own areas of experience. I give this one not because it is necessarily the most illustrative, but because it was in fact what pushed me into taking theology seriously.

So, with Matthew, apocalyptic language and all, we see that his three final parables have to do strictly with how to live in the time of Abel: first, being alert means preparing yourself patiently for the duration; secondly, the patient construction of the kingdom means having your imagination fixed on the abundant generosity of the One Who empowers and gives growth; and thirdly, what is demanded is a non-scandalized living out which is flexible enough to be able to recognize those whom the world is throwing out, and then a stretching out of the hand to create with them the kingdom of heaven. All of this is a making explicit of the eschatological imagination through the subversion from within of the apocalyptic imagination.

Now that we have read through the eschatological discourses in the Gospels we are in a good position to ask the question: in what does Christian hope consist? This will be the theme of our next and penultimate chapter.

Hope:
Where Boldness Blossoms
Out of Fear

I have been seeking to do two things thus far in these pages. The first was in relation to our understanding of God. That is, we investigated the way in which Jesus brought into existence a new perception of God, and we followed the process by which this perception began to produce a series of changes in the way the apostolic group understood various aspects of human reality. The second had to do with showing how this perception which Jesus had, his eschatological imagination, little by little subverted the apocalyptic imagination which marked his contemporaries and which tends, in other guises, to mark us and our contemporaries from within. In this way we began to enter into something of what Jesus understood by the kingdom whose arrival he was announcing, the kingdom born under the sign of the innocent victim, and to be able to understand the difference which this arrival caused to the time in which it has befallen us to live.

Now I would like to do something rather risky, which consists in asking about how we are related to all that has gone before, which is to ask in what it is licit for us to hope, as Christians at the end of the twentieth century. I say risky, because whoever begins to talk about themes which touch on our lives as we live them is allowing the bull to pass very close to the chest. My conception of theology is that this sort of bullfighting is the only style that convinces in the long run, even though it be less elegant and objective than other forms of luring the same bulls by. However, at the same time it is also more apparent how little he has to give who arrogates to himself the rôle of interpreting the word of God for others, how little the resistance he offers to those horns. But it is in vulnerability that theology lies....

ephobounto gar...For They Were Afraid

In the eighteenth chapter of the book of Genesis, Abraham receives the visit of three angels. The text is mysterious, since at times it refers to three persons and at times to the Lord. We are before a text where the primitive monolatry of the fertile crescent was still in the process of emerging. All of this matters little. What is important is that these visitors come shortly after God has promised to the ninety-nine year-old Abraham that he will be the father of a multitude of nations through a son, Isaac. This son would be born within a year to his wife, Sarah, old and barren, well past her menopause. In fact there was no natural possibility of such a happening. The angels, or the Lord, repeat to Abraham that they will return in the spring, and that Sarah will be with child. Sarah is listening from behind a flap in the tent and laughs out loud at hearing such an absurd promise. The visitor asks why she laughs, as if there were anything too hard for the Lord, and promises the child once more. Sarah denies having laughed, because she was afraid. In the Greek of the Septuagint "she was afraid" comes out as *ephobéthé gar*.

The impossible promise produces two reactions in her: laughter, on account of the absurdity of the promise, and fear, because of what is announced. After all, when one reaches a certain age, one is accustomed to being sorry for oneself to some degree for things not realized, even though one has built one's little security in the midst of what could be carried through. Someone comes along and with a solemn promise breaks that little security, thus threatening a future that is totally uncertain and quite different from anything one had imagined.

Let us jump to one of the most mysterious passages of the apostolic witness, the original ending to the Gospel of Mark. The women go to Jesus' tomb, the definitive symbol of impossibility. They are on their way to perform a pious act, proper to the sort of piety that characterizes the dominion of death: the anointing of a body. They are going to find a stone, an obstacle too great for their own slight strength and one which is going to make even this most elemental act of piety very difficult. However, they find the stone put aside and a young man who says to them:

> Be not affrighted: Ye seek Jesus of Nazareth, which was crucified: he is risen; he is not here: behold the place where they laid him. But go your way, tell his disciples and Peter that he goeth

before you into Galilee: there shall ye see him, as he said unto you. And they went out quickly, and fled from the sepulcher; for they trembled and were amazed: neither said they anything to any man; for they were afraid [*ephobounto gar*]. (Mark 16:6–8)

Nothing in the phrasing of the texts of the New Testament is accidental, and it seems to me that in the story of Sarah we have the reference which gives the context for the Marcan account of the frightened women.[1] The stone put aside and the absence of the corpse were not in the first instance a motive for rejoicing, but for terror. Terror because what had happened was quite outside anything that could be expected. Beside this, the possibility of the birth of a child to an aged lady is a mere nothing. Terror because now there was no security, no rules, nothing normal could be trusted in. And worse, terror because everything difficult and frightening which Jesus had taught had to begin to come about: he went before them, as he had told them.

It seems to me that here we have the most appropriate place from which to start our examination of hope. I want to focus on this because there is nothing pretty about Christian hope. Whatever Christian hope is, it begins in terror and utter disorientation in the face of the collapse of all that is familiar and well known.

Pretty Words amid Disturbing Reality

I have insisted throughout these pages on what Jesus came to announce: the absolute goodness, effervescence, creativity, power, aliveness, and so on, of God. Of the God who is without ambivalence, ambiguity, shade of death or violence. This not only is the God whom Jesus announced, but he wished to give a practical demonstration of this God who knows not death by handing himself over to death so as to expose and reveal the mechanism of death which dominates human culture and societies. I have tried to show that it was to create a belief in this God that Jesus came, in order to make it possible that in the midst of this world we might begin to live trusting in the love of this God, and thus to live as if death did not exist, constructing a counter-history which has no end.

---

1. I owe this insight, as many others, to J. D. M. Derrett, who points it out (with acknowledgment of his own source) in the prologue to his work *The Victim: The Johannine Passion Narrative Re-examined* (Shipston-under-Stour: Drinkwater, 1993).

Now, speaking about God in these terms is absolutely necessary, but by doing so we always run the risk of falling into words which are excessively pretty, and thus resoundingly hollow. It was not for nothing that Jesus wanted to speak to his own employing the normal language of his hearers, full as it was of the terminology and sentiments of violence to which they were accustomed. I think that it is here, with the frightened women fleeing from the empty tomb, that we can begin to understand how the vision of God which I have described and which seems so overly pretty, and the violent reality within which it was preached, come together, giving as a result what we call hope. The birth of Christian hope, like the coming of the kingdom, is a two-edged sword: on the one hand it offers life without end wrapped up in a loving God, and on the other it jerks the rug from beneath the feet of those who come into contact with it, removing the fragile but real security which is offered by life in the shadow of death.

Now, it seems to me that this element, the drastic nature of Christian hope, has to be approached with a good deal of care, because it is perfectly possible to confuse it with the drastic violence of a certain apocalyptic expectation, which is, I would say, very far from being the same thing. Allow me to explain: we have already seen in the apostolic witness the process of leaving behind the vision of the violent apocalyptic god who was to produce a decisive rupture in history, starting from which the good would be consoled and the bad punished. We saw that the apostolic witness itself understands this coming of God already to have happened, and to have happened as a human victim, and that from then on history runs its own course, and when it finishes, howsoever it finishes, it will be illuminated in reverse by the glory of the victim, when it will be understood who have been the sheep and who the goats.

We saw also that one of the temptations of the first Christians was to remain enclosed within the apocalyptic imagery, thinking in terms of a rapid, vengeful, and definitive return of Jesus to do away with this wicked generation. Well, if what you are hoping for is a rapid, rescuing arrival of God, where you will be saved and your enemies will perish horribly, this is, indeed, a certain sort of hope. It is an urgent and drastic hope; but what is hoped for is a rescue, and a violent rescue, carried out by an authority who comes down from on high to sort things out. If in the midst of this sort of expectancy you are called to keep your mind fixed on the things that are above, where the victim is risen at the right hand of God, what is apparently being asked of you is the sort of bravery that is asked of those who are on the deck of a sinking ship: to keep up their courage because the Coast Guard is on its way.

However, what we perceive in the apostolic witness is something a little different. As there develops the way in which the apocalyptic imagination is subverted from within, we see ever less insistence on hope and ever more on patience, so that in the letter to Titus we read the following:

> Tell the elders to be sober, grave, temperate, sound in faith, in charity, in patience. (Tit. 2:2)

That is to say, where Paul had spoken to the Corinthians in terms of faith, hope, and charity, now patience replaces hope.

Might this not merely be the disillusioned change of those who have lost their hope in the imminence of the second coming and for that reason are exhorting others to patience? Or might it be that patience here means something rather different?

What I would suggest is that the transformation of hope into patience corresponds exactly to the same process we have been seeing of the coming into existence of the eschatological imagination, and that in this transformation nothing is lost either of the drastic quality or of the urgency of the hope that was born with the resurrection of Jesus. However, that hope became structured from within in a quite different way. I will indicate what I understand with an invented example, which could be echoed in your own experience.

Imagine that you are in a highly conflictual situation, where a series of injustices are being perpetrated, and they are being covered up to protect people of power and influence. Since you now understand that God has nothing to do with death, that God is infinitely effervescent, creative, and so on, you begin, maybe with much fear and trembling, but you begin nonetheless, to speak the truth about the situation in which you find yourself, and in which you have been, or even are still, to some extent, complicit. You know that by doing this you are putting yourself at risk, you are beginning to cast light into dark places, and that this light will be strongly resisted by the interested parties. What gives you courage to appeal to the competent authorities is your belief that they can restore order to the situation, they can make justice prevail there where there is none, and you believe that you too will be vindicated for your action. The image which you have of God is that, effectively, God loves those who are in the process of being destroyed, annihilated by the violence of the situation, and for that reason God will indeed be on your side to bring the matter to a good end. You have a strong hope in God, and the surety, based on your faith in the resurrection of Jesus, that God is capable of intervening to change the situation.

So what happens? Effectively you assume the risks of exposing to the light of day what is going on, to the advantage of the weak, and trust that the relevant authorities, recognizing the justice of your cause, will intervene. But something rather different happens: the others have a thousand ways of making things look different, of discrediting your action, of convincing the authorities that the problem is your own and that without you all would be well. The authorities, instead of recognizing the justice of your cause, become very cautious, for they are really not too interested in intervening too strongly where there are so many instances of influence in play and where to intervene would be both drastic and a lot of hard work. So, in the long run, the authority doesn't back you up; rather, depending on the circumstances, either they allow you to be crushed or they get rid of you.

Exactly this was what happened to a friend of mine who worked in a prestigious jewelry firm in a Latin American republic, which I will not name, when she appealed, very discreetly, to the foreign owners of the firm to bring order to a series of frauds and injustices which she was witnessing. She ended up fired, and the usual crowd safe in their jobs.

You may have heard of the murders of street kids in Brazil, and especially in the region around Rio de Janeiro, the *baixada fluminense,* for they have made headlines around the world. But the story of how those stories began to see the light of day is very interesting: a Carioca[2] dancer appeared in the town hall, evidently with some difficulty and shame, to denounce his former lover of many years, a military policeman from the *baixada fluminense* for forming part of a death squad which was dedicated to what is called, in police slang, "burning the archives," that is, killing any street kids who might be witnesses to illegal police activity. He, the dancer, was no longer able to keep quiet about the matter. You can imagine, in the first place, how difficult it must have been for that dancer to make the denunciation on account of his relationship with the one he was implicating; secondly, how easy it would have been to ridicule such a denuncia-

2. "Carioca" is the adjective that describes an inhabitant of Rio de Janeiro.

tion, coming from the source it came from; and thirdly, how little the authorities wanted to hear the news, let alone take the appropriate measures. However, it was that wrenching act of bravery which began the process of bringing to light what no one wanted to know.[3] Such stories must abound in the memory and knowledge of all of you, for the recent history of this continent[4] is especially rich in them.

In such circumstances, what happens with hope? What we are seeing is that the God of the victims does *not* rush in to rescue the situation; there are no apocalyptic interventions where evil is uncovered and good stands vindicated. Whoever assumes the risk of bringing things to light, stands, more often than not, alone; and even when they do not, this is only thanks to the intervention of other people in solidarity. Here is where there is produced what is perhaps the most difficult and substantial of the changes in the perception of God which we have been seeing. The God of victims becomes present not as rescuer, but as the One who gives hope to persons so that they may themselves run the risk of becoming victims. The tender and kind-hearted Father, absolutely effervescent and vivacious, becomes present as the empowering of the subject to live the absolute twilight of being crushed when she casts light on dark places.

In this way hope suffers a sea change: it is no longer hope of a rescue, but a fixed surety of that which is not seen, where there seems to be no way out, and where death and its system seem absolutely dominant; and it is this fixed surety of that which is not seen which empowers us to the forging of a counter-history to that of the dominion of death. It is for this reason, I suggest, that the word "patience," and another, "perseverance," begin to appear in the development of the apostolic witness instead of "hope." To give an example: nowhere in the book of Revelation do the Greek words for hope, *elpis* and *elpidzō,* appear. However, there does appear, in significant contexts, the word *hupomoné* — patience, perseverance. It is not that hope is being abandoned, but rather that its inner structure is being discovered in the degree to which it is set free from the apocalyptic imagination. It is hope that empowers to bear the crushing violence of the world precisely because it keeps the mind fixed on the God who is revealed by the victim seated at the right hand of God. Patience means nothing else; it doesn't correspond to our banal use of

---

3. See G. Dimenstein, *A guerra dos meninos* (São Paulo: Brasiliense, 1990), an extraordinary work of investigative journalism. The dancer appears briefly on p. 39.

4. These pages were written in Chile for an audience comprised of people from various Latin American countries.

the word, but has its root in the same word as "passion," that is, suffering, undergoing. The inner structure of hope in the "generation" which was born with the frightening resurrection of Jesus is the empowerment to risk suffering to bring light to the world.

In this way we can see that hope has lost nothing of its drastic quality or of its urgency, but that it has been, it also, subverted from within, coming to be a fixing on what is absolutely not seen: the vindication of the victim in the midst of stories which apparently do not end well, and where it is only being fixed on the God who knows not death which allows us to imagine that the real story one day to be revealed will be very, very different, and that the lightning which will illuminate all will cast a very different light on the monotonous story which we know too well.

The Utterly "Other" and the World of Contradictions

One quality of the hope which flows very directly from this understanding is that hope is in no way a natural reality. There does exist a certain natural expectancy which we sometimes call "hope": for example, I have a cold, and I have the hope that in a week or so it will have gone, as usually happens. However, what I'm hoping for here is the natural development of a normal circumstance. Now imagine that you are in a car crash, and that you are trapped by the metal structure and cannot get out. You can see that there are flames, and that soon the flames will reach the fuel tank, then there will be an explosion, and you have no way of escaping the death which that explosion will cause. That is to say, there is no natural power of your own which will allow you to get through. Your impotence is absolute. The only hope of your coming out of this alive is if someone from without, someone who is not in the car, comes quickly and pulls you free.

Please forgive me the inadequacy of the image, for it too suggests an image of God as rescuer, an image which, as I have told you, I want to avoid. The reason why I use this image of powerlessness within a burning car is not to speak about the rescue, but about the *other*. The one hope you have in the face of death is a hope that rests on *another*, on one who is not in the car. I fear that this is too obvious to say, but it is sometimes the most obvious thing which is least perceived: there is no hope in the face of death and its dominion which is not hope in *another* who has nothing to do with death. There was a whole way of talking about hope as a certain confidence in the future, as if there were a hopeful dynamic within the development of history as such. That would be the "cold" model of history, something that will just get better: but to be in the face of death is not like having a cold. In the face of death and its dominion there is no hope at all unless I hope in another, totally different from me, someone who isn't in the car crash.

It is in the light of this that we must try to understand Jesus' preaching about God. He wasn't pruning God of violence as a sort of apology to us, so that we might think better of God: "Look, God isn't such a bad sort as you've thought." Nor was it so that we might have an idea of God as close by, tender-hearted, loving, and so on, however fundamental that may have been. Rather, it was completely indispensable that we should perceive that God is utterly *other* than ourselves. The shearing off the violence from the perception of God is vital for us to be able to understand that God is utterly *Other*, forming no part of our violent stories, and entering into no sort of rivalry with us. It is only thanks to the fact of being so totally other, so without possible rivalry or comparison with us, that God is capable of entering in a purely gratuitous, non-violent way into our story to empower us to learn to forge another story. We perceive something of this complete otherness of God in Matthew's insistence that God makes the sun to shine on good and bad alike and sends rain on both just and impious (Matt. 5:45). We see the same thing in the invitation to the banquet which the king gives for his son: the servants gathered in all whom they could find, good and bad alike (Matt. 22:10).

Well now, if God is so utterly other, and if God's ways are not our ways, God's goodness not our goodness, then the process of coming to hope in the one who is not inside the car, but who can pull us free, includes, *exactly in the degree to which our image of a rescuing God begins to collapse,* a very tough process of learning not to hope in ourselves. Part of the process of becoming aware of the utter otherness of God is the process of unhooking our hope from ourselves. Here I must tread very carefully so that what I say be not misunderstood. I'm not saying that we have to learn to despair in ourselves so that we can begin to hope — even though emotionally it may at times seem so — but that in the degree to which we come to learn to hope in the utter otherness of the Other, we can let go of the need we have to grasp onto something in ourselves which might be worthy of hope.

At root I am saying that our goodness or badness *does not matter,* and that hope in one who is utterly other has as one of its more important and profound effects a certain loss of preoccupation with our goodness or badness. The key here is that this being unpreoccupied with our own goodness or badness (which is nothing other than what has traditionally been called humility) is precisely what empowers us to act in a way that is fired by hope, and is creative of hope, in the violent circumstances of the world. And this is because we take for granted, maybe even with a certain relaxedness, that we are accomplices and participants in the dominion of the murderous lie, and yet are not scandalized by our complicity.

Let us return to the Matthean royal banquet: the servants have arrived, they have called you to the banquet, and there you go. On the way you start to turn over in your mind whether or not you're worthy to have been invited to that banquet, and frankly, you get all screwed up, because of your self-concern. You do not understand that the invitation does not discriminate among good and bad, and that you are being offered something which has nothing at all to do with questions of your worthiness or its lack, but is something quite different, purely gratuitous. If you do not understand this, you have remained within your own scandal at yourself: it is in that that consists your failure to put on the wedding garment which is freely offered to you, and because of this you remain silent when your host asks you why you have not put it on. The fact that you find yourself tied hand and foot afterward is nothing other than the logical working out of how tied up you've been all along.

Let us consider two more contemporary examples. As I see it, the reason that *Schindler's List* is the best lesson in moral theology that has reached a wide public in a long time is that Oskar Schindler *was not "good,"* nor concerned to be so. By being unconcerned about his own goodness, he was capable of constructing an extraordinary counter-story of hope in the very face of the most vertiginous example of the murderous lie. Now just imagine if he had sat around saying, "Well, I'm not a good enough sort of chap to do something demanding heroic sanctity, so I'd better take care of my little problems with alcohol and my libido, and when I've got those sorted out, I'll dedicate myself to doing works of charity among the Jews." He would have done nothing at all, and there would have been no Jews left among whom to do works of charity. In fact, thanks be to God, his deep complicity with evil (he started his factory to make money out of the war) did not prevent him from pulling off what has to be one of the most astounding *jeux d'esprit,* one of the most formidably creative exercises of the imagination of which our planet has record.

Let us imagine that our Carioca dancer was scandalized by the sort of relationship he had with his former lover (and the erotic and the violent are never very distant the one from the other, this being merely a little more transparent in the gay than in the "straight" world, but whoever doubts its presence in this latter might like to glance at how Shakespeare depicts the relation between Desdemona and her macho military hero husband, Othello). Let us imagine our dancer stuck within his scandal, saying to himself: "What I lived with him, and what he does to the street kids in the *baixada fluminense* are too similar, so I'd better get myself in order and make myself good before denouncing something in which I'm so profoundly complicit." He'd never have got around to denouncing what was going on. He would never have started to construct the wedding banquet of the risen victim.

All of this leads us to an indispensable dimension of the understanding of hope, which is that either it is hope *for me exactly and unconcernedly as I am* or it is not hope at all. Hope is indeed made present collectively, by the public announcement — which the Church tries constantly to make present — of the absolutely loving aliveness of God and by Jesus' imitable creation of a belief in that death-lessness. But hope is not something general; it is not satisfied with saying, "Here is good news for humanity, and that thanks to this announcement all will end well with humanity." It says quite specifically that this news is good *for me* just as an accomplice and participant in all the scandals of humanity. It says that you, just as you are, are invited to create the wedding banquet of the slaughtered lamb, not in spite of being who you are, but exactly as who you are, warts and all.

I hope that it is not necessary to say how important this is for our moral living. It means that it is taken for granted that there is no actualization by us of goodness, no participation in the process of bringing light to the dark places, in the forging of the celestial counter-story, that starts from some cleanness of ours. And it is in the context of this understanding that it turns out to be so important that we understand why Jesus described the Holy Spirit as the Counsellor for the Defense. Not only because the Defender will reveal and vindicate the innocence of the victims which the world creates, but because the Defender defends us against our own bad conscience, making us see that we can indeed create the celestial counter-story, and that we are not to be held up by our effective complicity in evil. With this we draw close to an insight proper to the most traditional Catholic moral theology, which says that we can never have an absolute certainty of having acted well in such or such a circumstance, because the good is only wrought in hope. This is the equivalent of saying that only those who are unpreoccupied by their own goodness or evil are really free to build what is good and probably have little idea that that is what they are doing. This because they know full well that they can't understand very well, let alone systematize, the counter-story which they are helping to bring about and whose full sense is yet to be revealed.

All of this has been to say that the notion of God's absolute alterity, that God be utterly Other, and the notion that hope is good *for me*, are completely inseparable. It is only thus that the true God, not the rescuer from difficult situations, but the one who empowers revealing passions, gives us the capacity to construct the counter-story that has nothing to do with death.

Introducing an Element
Both Subtle and Important . . .

Almost everything that I have said in the previous section could have been said by a Protestant theologian, and probably better than by me, for we have been looking at what they call "justification by faith" and not by works, which is the central axis of their confession and of their protest.[5] From time to time it does us Catholics a great deal of good, immersed as we too often are in an atrocious moralism, to grasp the force of this teaching. However, something is missing from it. You could understand what I've just been saying as follows: God, as a good observer, has despaired of our capacity to be good, and so has decided to offer us, by means of Jesus' coming, an unbreakable confidence in his absolute goodness toward us, so that we can cease to be worried about being good or bad, and, fixing our trusting gaze on God, we can live our life without fear, for we have been invited to

---

5. Faith and hope tend to come intertwined in the Reformed presentation, so that what is understood by faith is something much closer to what we understand by hope. That is, they emphasize the element of faith which consists in a confident resting in God's love, the subjective element of faith. Catholic theologians tend rather to highlight faith in its dimension of the knowledge of the absolute and unambiguous goodness and lovingkindness of God, reserving the more subjective element for the treatise on hope.

the banquet, where we will be given a wedding garment which will cover up what we really are.

Well, that is *not* what I was trying to say. It seems to me that hope offers us something more than this. We begin, yes indeed, in the position of those who are to a greater or lesser extent complicit in the murderous lie, and we are all, to some degree, scandalized by ourselves. That is, we are all formed from within by a rivalistic mimetic desire, by which we grasp our identity, our security, in an envious and violent way with respect to other people, or the social "other." The desire which forms our "I," the desire by which we receive and grasp our "I," has already introduced all of us into the world of scandal. The root question is: does God simply accept us in our scandal, giving us the confidence to live in the midst of our scandalized state? Or could it be that the very same desire which forms us in the scandal of mimetic complicity is capable of being transformed into another sort of desire, a pacific desire, neither envious nor scandalized? The same questions asked in another way would look like this: does God accept that the stories which we humans are forging with our lives are murky, violent stories and decide, nevertheless, to produce certain sparks in our midst of a celestial counter-story, and then to reveal at the end what has really been going on all along without our having much idea of what that will be like, so utterly "other" will it be, so totally different are God's ways from our ways?[6] Or could it be that in the midst of our murky and complicitous stories, God's acceptance of our condition as people-in-scandal works by being the place that allows us to begin to forge with our lives, and knowingly, something of the counter-story, so that when all is revealed at the end, something of a continuity will be seen between what we thought we were doing and what we will there see in fullness?

You have already seen that, although I allow the horns of Protestantism to graze me very closely, my bullfight remains obstinately Catholic. All the difference is made by the fact that Jesus came to create a belief as something truly and humanly imitable. That is, when he gave us his revealing passion as a model for us to construct stories in flexible imitation of his own, he was at the same time making it possible for our rivalistic human desire to be transformed into pacific desire, in imitation of the pacific desire of God, which we normally call God's love. That is to say: if hope allows us to become unpreoccupied by our scandal, by our complicity, if it allows us to enter

---

6. The parable of the sheep and the goats could be read in this way.

into that continual process of being absolved of our bad conscience by the Defending Spirit, it does this in the degree to which it empowers us, in fact, and starting exactly where we are, to create a story like Jesus' own, even though in our cases these be much more ambiguous than his. A story of living as if death were not, thus enabling us to forge the story of the innocence of others, victims, even if we are destroyed in the process.

Here is what is important: that counter-story, which no one manages to forge with absolute limpidity, is not the story of Jesus superimposed on our own, but it really is *our* story. However, it is so not as a story grasped by us, something we know we have done and of which we can be proud, brandishing it before God as our very own; rather it is exactly our hope in God's creative vivaciousness which allows us *not* to grasp onto our story, but to allow God to create, by means of us, something much richer and more extraordinary than we could imagine that we are about. Let us say this in another way. I imagine myself in the situation of the Carioca dancer, or of Oskar Schindler, and, with a much greater stretch of the imagination, I picture myself having the courage to act as they acted and I do so, since I have a basic grasp of the faith, with some notion that I am doing this hoping that the God who does not know death will know how to bring something of light out of my action, even if no one is aware of it at the time. Well, I'm not *only* hoping that God will not take into account how little worthy I am to be presented before the heavenly throne. That is, I'm not only unworried about my goodness or badness, but my very hope includes hoping that God will know how to work it that *this* story, which I have so fumbled in forging, be *my* story, and that at the end, the "I," the life story which subsists without end, will be read from this my somewhat muddled and complicated attempt to forge the story of the victim; and that at the end it will in fact be "I," an "I" that is hard to recognize for sure, who will be so read.

Hope means that none of us have access to what our story is; we cannot wield it, grasp it, make a presentation of it. Rather it means that, in the face of death, whether in its physical form or in the form of its violent and expulsive dominion, we hope that we will receive an "I" in whose formation we have begun to participate, once we have become unhooked from our old story. We always receive ourselves from what is other than us, whether that other be violent or loving; but, as we begin to receive ourselves from the loving Other, in the form of our empowerment to construct a counter-story in the face of

death, it genuinely is ourselves that we receive, and the story really
will be ours. I think that this is exactly what John is saying, far more
beautifully and succinctly, when he says:

> Beloved, we are already children of God, although it does not
> yet appear what we shall be: but we know that when Jesus ap-
> pears and we see him as he is, we will be like him. Whosoever
> has placed this hope in Jesus is purified, so as to be pure as he
> is. (1 John 3:2–3)

That is, we are already children of God, with all our scandalized living out, but we do not know our identity, and we cannot grasp it:
it is eschatological, and we will receive it in fullness when the whole
story inaugurated by Jesus stands revealed. Those who have placed
this hope in Jesus, that is, have become unhooked from their identity
in order to receive it from the flexible imitation whose fullness will
be revealed at the end, all they are being purified, made really different, so that their desire will be transformed into that desire bereft
of scandal, that love without rivalry, in which consists the purity of
Jesus. We find something similar in the greatest theologian of the
nineteenth century, Fyodor Dostoyevsky, in his *Summa, The Brothers
Karamazov,* when Father Zosima gives this spiritual exhortation:

> What seems to you to be evil in you is purified by the mere fact
> of having noticed it.... At the moment when you see with terror
> that, in spite of your efforts, not only have you not drawn closer
> to your goal, but you have even drawn further away from it, at
> that moment, I warn you beforehand, you will reach your goal,
> and you will see above you the mysterious power of the Lord,
> who, unbeknownst to you, has guided you with love.[7]

Hope as the Rupture in the System

In the light of all this we can begin to understand Christian hope
as an unexpected rupture in the system. What do I mean by system? *Every* system. As humans we all live and inscribe our lives
within a series of systems, of games whose rules we know and to
which we adapt ourselves to a greater or a lesser extent. By "the

---

7. Quoted by R. Girard in *Critiques dans un souterrain* (Paris: Grasset, 1983), 135.

system" I mean every way of ours of having a story, of organizing our thinking and acting, every way of forging our lives and of
talking about them as something sure. And this system is, for many
people, most of the time, quite livable. It is moved neither by great
hopes nor shaken by great despairs. However, as I have tried to show
throughout these pages, every story, insofar as it is grasped, is a system structured by the murderous lie, whose security depends on some
exclusion. That is, every system is dominated and shaded by the definitive impossibility which comes from death, the impossibility of
moving the stone.

In the midst, then, of every system of ours, hope appears *not* as
the escape route from a cul-de-sac, nor as the fulfillment and embel-
lishment of what we already live, but as an unexpected rupture in
the system. It is a door open where all appeared to be closed, but
not the door open where we would like it to be, as the consoling
confirmation of our little hopes; rather it is exactly where we have a
tendency not to look, the gate of the victim. And at the moment that
it is that gate, small and not very attractive, which stands open, the
door of the victim risen and seated at the right hand of God, an unexpected rupture is produced in the system. It means that there is no
secure, grasped, story, not entirely satisfactory, but not wholly without its satisfactions. The fissure in the system is a terrible shaking up
because, exactly at the same time as it offers an unexpected way out
from the system, it casts a much more drastic and terrifying light on
it than what we had perceived before. It is in this context, and I suspect that only in this context, that it is possible to understand well
the Christian discourse about hell.

What I am suggesting is that at the moment when the risen victim
took his seat on the right hand of God — the vision of the Ascension,
which was the act of opening heaven up for us as the humanly realiz-
able story of the banquet of the slaughtered lamb — at that very same
moment, hell was opened up. In the same way in which the concept
of "heaven" was forever and definitively altered by Jesus' Ascension,
the same shake to the system revealed that the grinding on and on of
the system had depths far more horrendous and terrifying than had
been thought.

Now, precisely since this matter is highly scandalous, perhaps the
most scandalous of those we have looked at thus far, I want to tread
its terrain with a great deal of care. Please allow me to say in the
first place what I do *not* mean. The commonly held understanding
of hell remains strictly within the apocalyptic imagination, that is, it

is the result of a violent separation between the good and the evil worked by a vengeful god. It seems to me that if hell is understood thus, we have quite simply not understood the Christian faith; and the Christian story, instead of being the creative rupture in the system of this world, has come to be nothing less than its sacralization. That is, the good news which Jesus brought has been quite simply lost.

Let us apply the same way of understanding the coming into existence of the eschatological imagination as the subversion from within of the apocalyptic imagination which we have used up until now, and we will see that we come to understand hell in a rather different way. The doctrine of hell comes to be a quite indispensable part of the inner structuring of Christian hope. I'll try to show how by considering the most famous theological attempt to suppress hell: the doctrine of the *apokatastasis,* or final recapitulation of all things, a doctrine attributed to Origen.[8] According to this doctrine, there may be a last judgment, and after it, a separation of the good from the evil for an indefinite glory or condemnation, but that, at the very, very end, so kind and merciful is God that even the sinners in hell are able to be converted, so that all turns out well.

The problem with this explanation lies in the fact that *it is a system.* That is, it is a story already told, with its beginning, its moment of high drama, and its happy ending. And, like every system, exactly because it is a system, it suppresses hope. It is not necessary to hope during this life, because we already know the end of the story, so that the details of this story *don't matter.* Those of us who have made the journey from Cochabamba to La Paz[9] by bus know that the way is somewhat dangerous, with many curves, many precipices, little space for passing, and danger, above all in the rainy season, of landslides. The doctrine of the *apokatastasis* says: "it doesn't matter how the driver drives, because we will in any case get to La Paz. If he drives very quickly, and goes over one of the curves, it really doesn't matter, for we know beforehand that there are magic vicuñas[10] which, with angelic wings, will stop the bus in its plunge, bear it up, and return it to the road, so that we will, in any event, get to La Paz." The result of conceiving the journey from Cochabamba to La Paz in this way cannot but be much more dangerous than the conception held, thank

---

8. Origen's own version of this was probably so nuanced that it could not justly be called a system. As so often it is the "school of" which hardens a fluid, open-ended way of thinking into a system.

9. Both cities are situated at different altitudes of the Bolivian Andes.

10. Small quadrupeds of the llama family.

heavens, by the majority of the bus drivers, according to which the route is dangerous and the curves and the weather conditions should be treated with all due respect.

What I want to conclude from these speculations drawn from the Andean cosmovision is this: if there is a total system, a story already known, then there is no hope. If there is hope of leaving the system, then at the very same time its counterpart comes into being, the possibility of not leaving the system. But once you have glimpsed that it is possible to leave the system, then you have also seen how much more horrifying is the system than what you had thought before, and thus, how much more smartly must you walk to leave it behind.

If we look at it in this way, we can begin to draw some conclusions about how to conceive of hell in a way that is outside the apocalyptic imagination within which it is commonly presented. In the first place hell can *never* be considered a threat *for other people;* such a presentation remains absolutely within a discourse of vengeance by which a preacher, or whoever, unloads personal ire against those whom that speaker dislikes, and who are in all probability very like the speaker (for we tend to fear and to hate those disconcertingly like us rather than those who are strikingly different). Secondly, hell must be considered a possibility *for me* and not for others, but *only in the degree to which I begin to acquire the audacity to construct the counter-story in the face of this world* and begin to detect the consequences, in all their depth, of my complicity in its contrary. This word "possibility" is very important, because it is not the word "threat": the accusing threat creeps up on one who has no defense attorney. The real "possibility" remains there as a description of the real consequences of what I am in the process of leaving behind, thanks to the Attorney who makes it possible that even this person, scandalized by my complicity in the reign of death, should have the boldness to imagine that I am being empowered to construct a hope-fired counter-story of a fullness yet to be conceived. This, I think, is the understanding of hell to be found in one of the greatest theologians of the seventeenth century, Pedro Calderón de la Barca, presented in a work whose suggestive title is "The One Who Was Damned through Lack of Trust."[11]

With this we can say, as Hans Urs von Balthasar observed, that hell exists, as the Church has always maintained; nevertheless it is perfectly possible that there be nobody at all there. More than that: it

---

11. *El condenado por desconfiado* in the original.

is perfectly legitimate for us to hope, in the strictest theological sense, and pray that there be nobody there. However, our attitude must be to *hope,* and not to take for granted, that hell stays empty. Would God that Origen's profound intuition turns out to be right, and that at the end all manner of things are well for everybody and that even the most obstinate of Cains have learned to accept the forgiveness of our Abels. But there is a great difference between hoping in this possibility and suppressing hope by taking it for granted. It seems to me that this is the deep sense of one of the Church's most beautiful feasts, All Souls, the day of the dead, more so if it is understood as the day on which we pray especially for those with no one to pray for them, those who died despairing, the forgotten, those who left behind memories of hate and of resentment, those who everyone would like to see burn eternally.

Back to the Frightened Women

We began with the women who rushed fleeing from the fissure in the system, from the empty tomb, and did not dare to say anything to anybody. I've tried to give some sense to their fear as the place from which hope is born. For, at one go, heaven was being opened, hope was being born from a rupture in impossibility, from an unexpected and unimaginable breach, and the rug was being pulled from under the feet of all our little securities, our hopes ritualized in the shadow of death. There was opening up the space of a new and unheard of drastic quality which could never have existed in the pagan world (it is enough to read some funerary inscriptions from pagan Rome to see this), and which, once born, can never be suppressed. Nothing has been able to stay the same since the resurrection of the innocent victim, much though we might want to slip into reverse.

However, for Christian hope to be born, the fear which the women experienced had to be filled out with the vision which we associate with the Ascension, the vision of heaven open, with the victim seated at the right hand of God. That vision of the open heaven with the risen victim had to force its way through the apocalyptic imagination so that hope might be displaced from fixation on a rescuing god and relocated in a God who empowers the building of heaven in un-imagined ways by enabling us to fix our minds on the things that are above. In the same way, the vindictive coming of the Son had to be transformed into the rupture in the here and now produced by the many comings of the victim as forgiveness, around which we learn to construct patient stories. So we come to see in the texts of the apostolic witness the development of two new realities: at the same time as the conception of hope which I have been trying to sketch out matures, there is born an insistence in the importance of a certain bold freedom of speech — *parrhesía*. This bold frankness of speech, so recommended in the epistle to the Hebrews (which is itself, all of it, an exhortation to hope), has nothing to do with the arrogance of those who denounce because they know they are right. It is a new and unheard of audacity, absolutely and intrinsically linked to the good news: a freedom in speaking and in revealing what is hidden and covered over that is powered by the hope that even the one who is speaking is being enabled to leave behind complicity in what is being denounced. The justified fear of the women is being transformed by hope in the mercy of the forgiving victim.

At the same time there develops a strong insistence on asking that the Lord come, not the avenger, but the forgiving victim who is at the door knocking so that we might let him in (Rev. 3:20). The one who is at the door is not necessarily at the door we would have liked him to be at, but more probably at the door of our vulnerability, at the door we try to keep shut to cover over our scandal, both personal and social. The last chapter of the New Testament revolves around the Lord's promise that he is coming and our insistent request that he come: Maran-atha — come Lord! Christian hope consists precisely in our daring to ask with insistence that the forgiving victim become present to us, inviting us to his banquet, as one who burrows a hole in our hut, arriving like a thief in the night, so that we don't miss through sleep the wrenching invitation to build the celestial counterstory in the teeth of death.

With this we can see something of how the time of prayer and liturgy was born — the insistent request that the forgiving victim come, repeated throughout the time which has come to be called "ordinary," the time in which we seek the ways in which the sacraments and signs of that coming inflame our hearts to dare to say, with all that it implies, what those first early risers were unable to say, *ephobounto gar,* for they were afraid....

Chapter 9 _____

The Marriage of the Lamb
Has Come...

Up till this point we have tried to follow the inner dynamic of the apostolic witness to understand something of the imagination that was opened up by the life, death, and resurrection of Jesus, an imagination which I have called "eschatological." It is above all an imagination which nurtures and empowers life in the midst of the violence and contradictions, our own and others', in which we live. In this way I have tried to fill out something of what the apostolic witness means by calling us to have our mind fixed on the things that are above. We will be coming back to this before we're through. There remains, however, an element which, up until now has not received much emphasis and which is in a sense the most important thing of all: heaven. We have seen heaven under its active form, so to speak: that is, the creation of stories which are to subsist forever, stories created in hope by improbable people who hope to be recognized in them when all stands revealed. But that is only a part of the matter, and perhaps not the most important part. The apostolic witnesses give us a series of hints about what we might call the "receptive" part of heaven, that is, the part which has to do with "being recognized," and which has got to be, by far, the most important part. After all:

> Herein is love, not that we loved God, but that God loved us and sent his Son to be the propitiation for our sins.
>
> (1 John 4:10)

With this in mind we are going to look at some of the hints about the "receptive" experience of heaven, hints whose purpose is further to empower us for the small creative part which is our own.

179

Reputation and Shame

When the apostolic witness speaks of heaven, of the manifestation of God, or of the coming of the Son, there is always a word added, and it is the word "glory." This word has become popularized in phrases like "May God have her in his glory," this being understood as synonymous with "May she rest in peace." I would like to concentrate a little on this word "glory," because it is much more interesting and informative than it might seem at first sight. Our word "glory" translates the Greek word *doxa*, whose basic meaning is opinion or reputation.

Let us see how this works by looking at two different ways of translating some verses from John's Gospel:

> I receive not glory from men. But I know you, that ye have not the love of God in you. I am come in my Father's name, and ye receive me not: if another shall come in his own name, him ye will receive. How can ye believe, which receive glory one of another, and seek not the glory that cometh from God only?
>
> (John 5:41–44)

Thus the Authorized version, slightly altered (I have replaced "honor" with "glory'). Now let us paraphrase it like this:

> I do not receive my reputation from other humans, but I know that, at heart, you do not love God. For I have come representing God's person, and you pay no attention to me. If another were to come, with no more authority than his own, you would have no difficulty in receiving what he had to say. How can you believe in the One God if you depend for your reputation on your imitation of each other and do not seek the reputation which God alone can give?

Not only do we lose nothing of the original in the paraphrase, but Jesus' logic becomes much clearer to us. He takes it for granted that we, as human beings, depend absolutely on someone other to give us our sense of worth. That is, at root we all have a profound need that someone should recognize us, and how we act is deeply motivated by our need to obtain such recognition. We all need that someone should take note of us and tell us "I have noticed you, and I like what you are doing." The problem which Jesus raises with his listeners is the same question that we have seen in other circumstances: on which "other" do I depend to be noticed and told "I like you"?

I think that there are two possibilities: I can depend entirely on my peers, in which case my goodness, my striving to do well, and the sort of life I lead will be a reflection of them, and I'll have to do everything to keep myself well considered by them, receiving those whom they receive and excluding those whom they exclude, so as not to run the risk of finding myself the excluded one. Not only all these things, which might seem superficial, like the little games of hypocrisy which we all have to play to keep our social life going, but it is also the case, perhaps without my realizing it, that all my "I" is nothing other than a construction forged by the difficult game of keeping my reputation. There is no other "I" at the bottom of it all, behind the "I" which I am acquiring through the little manipulations by which I search to keep my reputation. My "I" and my way of being related to the "other" are the same thing.

The other possibility is that I receive my "I" from God, and here's the rub: God has an awful reputation. Which is nothing other than saying that God's reputation and the reputation of the victim are the same thing. That is what Jesus was suggesting: in order to receive your reputation, your being noticed and recognized, by God, you have to be prepared to lose the reputation which comes from the mutually reinforcing opinion and high regard of those who are bulwarks of public morality and goodness and find it among those who are held as nothing, of no worth. That is also what Paul says to the Corinthians:

> God chose what is weak in this world to put to shame what is strong; God chose what is base and despised, even things that are not, to bring to nothing the things that are. (1 Cor. 1:27–28)

Now the couplet "glory," or reputation, and "shame" appear throughout the apostolic witness, never very far from one another. Let us see some examples: in the Lucan parable of the wedding banquet, the one who sits in a higher position is put to shame, while the one who sits in a lowly place is publicly recognized by the host, who says:

> "Friend, come higher." Thus will you receive glory in the face of the other guests. (cf. Luke 14:8–11)

In a place as different from Luke as 1 Peter, we read:

> If someone suffers as a Christian, let them not be ashamed, but
> let them glorify God in this name. (1 Pet. 4:16)

That is, the shame suffered as a consequence of building the story of
the victim *is* the way by which we give a just reputation to God. This
couldn't be clearer in a passage of the Gospel which is certainly an
authentic word of Jesus, for it reappears in various places in slightly
differing guises:

> For whosoever is ashamed of me and of my words in this adul-
> terous and evil generation, of that one will the Son of man
> also be ashamed when he comes in the glory of his Father with
> the holy angels. (Mark 8:38; Luke 9:26; cf. also Matt. 10:33;
> Luke 12:9)

So we see here that it is not only a matter of insisting on how we are
to give glory to God, being prepared to construct a tale of ill repute
in imitation of the one who was numbered among the transgressors,
but that one of Jesus' preferred ways of speaking about heaven itself
is in terms of receiving the glory, or reputation, which comes from
God. Heaven will be a superabundance of a glorious reputation, the
recognition with high praise of the life story that has been built by
the one who was not ashamed to act in flexible imitation of the Son.

If we return to the passage from John with which we began, we
can now see exactly how glory works: the order of this world has its
own glory, which depends on mutually rivalistic imitation, and is a
glory or reputation that is grasped and held on to with difficulty. Being enveloped in the order of this world prevents us from beginning
to act in solidarity with those of poor repute, because if we do so we
lose our reputation. But those whose minds are fixed on the things
that are above, that is, those who have begun to receive their "I"
from their non-rivalistic imitation of Jesus, already begin to derive
their reputation from the Father and not from their peers. This they
do in the degree to which, doubtless with much difficulty, they learn
to give little importance to the reputation which people give them
and thus become free to associate with those who have no reputation,
just like the one who was numbered among the transgressors.

If they manage not to be ashamed of what the world treats as
despicable, then, when the final revelation of the Son of man with
angels appears, when it will be established beyond doubt who God
really is, that is, when the risen victim is the central axis of all the life
stories that are under construction, then, at that moment those who

were little concerned about the loss of their reputation will receive an everlasting reputation: they will hear in the midst of a huge public what every little child wants to hear from its parents: "That's right, little one, that's what I wanted; I like what you've done."

This was well understood in antiquity, for St. Augustine's definition of glory is "Clara cum laude notitia,"[1] that is, being publicly pointed out, noticed, with praise. And this is to be understood not only as a public recognition of what has been achieved, as if God were a headmistress distributing end-of-term prizes; rather, that welcoming, peaceable, loving recognition by the "Other" re-creates the "I," reconstructs me. Just as my earthly "I" can remain formed by my grasping on to the reputation which comes from others who are, ultimately, in rivalry with me, so being seen and appreciated by the pacific other literally gives me my true "I," a "self" alive even when half buried beneath the rubble of the many wrong turnings which have been part of my attempt to re-create the celestial counter-story of the victim in the midst of the gossip and the squabbles of this world.

However, all this is not enough; our worldly quest for reputation, for glory, is more complex, and more subtle, than what might be understood if we left the matter here. I have been emphasizing things in a way which is faithful to the apostolic witness, but which doesn't take into account one of the developments in the human quest for reputation which has come to be possible thanks exactly to the slow coming into existence of the notion that the victim might be innocent. Let me explain. What I said might be understood to be suggesting that a good reputation in this world comes from a perverse order of things, and anybody who perceives how hypocritical this order is can very easily leave behind the good reputation, harvesting a bad reputation for oneself, scandalizing people a bit. Then, on being rejected by the guardians of public morality, one has the luxury of feeling that one is a victim, and thus deserving of a special glory all one's own.

I'm talking about the strategy for the self-canonization of the victim, and we can see this at work more or less throughout the whole spectrum of society. One of the ways of making yourself feel "special" is to adopt the rôle of someone with a bad reputation. We see this in the formation of religious sects, where it is their very forging of frontiers "over against" society, their own way of wanting to be

---

1. *Contra Maximinum* 2:13 and 40:22, quoted by J. Pieper in *Love* (available to me in the Spanish compilation *Las virtudes fundamentales* [Madrid: Rialp, 1980], 458).

"different," which produces a rejection from society. This leads the sect members to feel especially close to the Lord, because they have, after all, managed to get themselves persecuted for being Christians, so they must be the real thing. However, we don't have to look outside the Catholic Church to see similar mechanisms at work: certain groups in the Church, not without influence, proceed in just the same way. By seeking to distinguish themselves from others they provoke a rejection, which confirms them in their notion that they are especially necessary and opportune for the Church: the self-canonization of the self-victim. Rejection is courted so that one be cast as the ill-comprehended prophet and martyr.

It almost goes without saying that the same mechanism is at work in almost all so-called "minority" groups within society. What happened, for example, among gay groups at the time of the beginning of emancipation, traditionally attributed to the uprising against a police raid on the Stonewall bar in 1969,[2] was exactly the same thing: the emphasis of all that seems most bizarre and shocking in gay life was the consolidation of victim-status *by buying into a bad reputation*. The self-canonization of the self-victim. Thank God there has been no shortage of self-criticism of this tendency within gay culture itself, coming from people who only want to be thought of as just another human being: a pacific part of an "us," and not an "us" defined violently over against an oppressive and hypocritical "them."[3] The same process can be detected in almost all social groups demanding rights and probably in the relational history of all of us to a greater or lesser extent.

Well, in all the above cases we detect the same mechanism: we have the self-canonization of those who grasp at their reputation as "good" and do everything possible, even with recourse to violence, to paper over the little slips and scandals which might cause them to lose their reputation; and we have the mirror image, the enemy twin, of this: the self-canonization of those who glory in being considered "damned" and reject any attempt to suggest to them that, when all is said and done, they're not very different from

---

2. A police raid on the Stonewall bar, a gay bar in New York, on June 28, 1969, was successfully resisted, to the surprise both of the police and of those resisting. This incident has become the symbolic date for the beginning of the public refusal of gay people to be treated as less than human and is celebrated each year in many countries throughout the world.

3. For two recent and contrasting positions on this matter see B. Bawer, *A Place at the Table* (New York: Poseidon, 1993), and M. Signorile, *Queer in America* (New York: Random House, 1993).

anybody else. I hope that it can be seen that, in fact, the same mechanism is at work: we receive glory, reputation, "one of another," be that by rivalistic imitation, be it by a contrast violently provoked.

The fact is this: there is no difference between self-justification as "good" and self-abasement as "wicked." They are two oscillations of the same sort of desire and, it might be added, two oscillations which typically occur in the life story of the same person. With this we have returned to where we were in our discussion of hope. The glory, the reputation, which comes from God must be received and not grabbed. The Father's glory which is to be revealed at the coming of the Son of man with angels will be received by those who are deeply unpreoccupied about their reputation, their glory. The business of having a "good" or a "bad" reputation couldn't matter less, for both human goodness and human evil are social constructions shot through with rivalistic desire, with the desire which forges identity over against the "other." The glory of heaven, the recognition which re-creates, is not given by the mere fact of having garnered for oneself a reputation as a rejectable transgressor in this world, but is given to those who, on account of their unconcern about their reputation according to the glory of this world have been able to stand loose from what is thought of them as they grow in solidarity with *things that are not.* Loss of reputation is indeed the beginning of a life in accord with the Gospel, but that reputation is lost as in a fit of absence of mind by someone who doesn't really mind very much, not by someone who strives for self-canonization, adopting the rôle of one to be cast out. Heavenly reputation, glory, is given to one who doesn't really understand why she is receiving it, one who considers herself an unprofitable servant (Luke 17:10).

Beyond the Desire of Being Desired by Another...

There is still something missing in our meditation on glory, and, as always, it is something which we could apparently leave out without much loss, but which, as I see it, makes all the difference. It is this: when we treat of glory in its sense of "reputation," and when we understand that, in fact, what we all want is that someone say to the little child within, "That's fine, little one," we might remain within an understanding of our desire, of the deepest human yearning, as if what were definitive about our desire is that someone else should desire us. If desire is understood thus, Christian life would only be a matter of switching that "someone else." That is, empowered by our faith in the Other who has no worldly reputation, we can change parties, learning to receive our "I" not from the rivalistic human "other," but from the divine, pacific Other. So far, so good. The fixing of the mind on the things that are above would be the fixation on the One who really loves me and whose desire satisfies me, as opposed to those whose desires never satisfy me and tend to form me in violence and in rejection.

However, is it really the case that our deepest desire is the desire to be desired by another? Here we have one of the great differences between the thought of Hegel, who would have replied "yes," and that of Girard, whom I follow, who says "no." According to Girard the desire of being desired is one of the permutations of desire, and doubtless one which is very deeply present in our lives, but it does not exhaust what human desire is. Human desire is, in the first place, as we saw in our first chapter, desire *according to* the desire of another. That means that we are truly re-created not merely by sitting face-to-face with someone who loves us absolutely and pacifically, but that that love re-creates us *in the degree to which it suggests into being in us a desire in imitation of itself,* in which we are summoned into loving someone else, as that love loves them. It is this new imitation of the one who is loved which produces the new "I."

For this reason it is so important that, in the apostolic witness, the open heaven is not only a vision of *God,* before whom we are called to be seated so as to receive love, in a sort of eternal *tête-à-tête,* but it is a vision of the Son of man, the risen victim, seated at God's right hand. By means of this vision we are called to imagine something further yet. Glory, our being recognized with praise, is a dynamic thing which is created in the measure of our learning to imitate the desire of the Father for the Son. The desire which is called forth in us is not a linear thing which rests in the Father, in imitation of the Father's love resting in us, without more to it. The real way in which the Father provokes in us the desire that is love is by pointing us to his Son as the one whom he loves (cf. Mark 9:7 and other similar verses), so that we imitate the Father in this love. This love does not end in the Son, but the Son himself, as risen victim, points out to us and enfleshes for us, precisely in his rôle as risen self-giving victim, what the Father's love for humanity looks like and is, so that we may imitate it.

I know that this, which is the difference between an unnuanced monotheism and the trinitarian monotheism which we confess, is very dense. Allow me to climb the same summit by a different face. If glory were merely the revelation of the real reputation of the child who has fought hard in solidarity with victims in the midst of our world, then there would still be traces of the apocalyptic imagination present: we would be imagining a final and glorious vindication. But the one who is seeking to be vindicated still has not left behind the quest for a reputation received from the violent "other." She still needs to compare herself triumphantly with those who in life despised her.

I'm trying to sketch out something much more interesting: in the measure that we learn unconcern about our reputation, in that measure the Father can produce in us the same love which he has for his Son and the same love which he and his Son have for the human race. Here is where we have to make an imaginative effort, or at least I do. That love is in no way marked by any desire for vindication, for restoring besmirched reputations, for turning the tables of this world, and all that might seem to us to be just and proper, given the horror of the violence of our world. That love *loves* all that! It loves the persecutors, the scandalized; it loves the depressives and the traitors and the finger pointers. That love doesn't seek a fulminating revelation of what has really been going on as a final vengeance for all the violence, even though we may fear that it will be so. That love is utterly removed from being party to any final settling of accounts. That love, the love which was the inner dynamic of the coming of the Son to the world, of Jesus' historical living out, seeks desperately and insatiably that good and evil may participate in a wedding banquet.

This means that it is the mind fixed on the things that are above which allows the heart to be re-formed in the image of the Father's love, forgiving the traitors, the executioners, the persecutors, the weak, those gone astray, not on account of some ethical demand, or to obey some commandment, but quite simply because they are loved, they are delighted in. When Luke has Jesus on the cross say, "Father, forgive them for they know not what they do" (Luke 23:34), he was not only depicting a Jesus who was effectively revealing the mechanism of death, which includes the blindness of its participants as to what they are doing, nor was it an ethical imperative that Jesus should forgive them so that he might go to his Father "clean'; rather it was just that, in truth, and without any remorse or sadomasochism,[4] Jesus loved his slayers.

This means that when we are able to stand loose from our reputation and, because of that, from our need to insist on a day of reckoning, the eschatological imagination, the mind fixed on the things that are above, begins to give us the capacity to love human beings without any sort of discrimination, in imitation of that love, quite without rivalry, which the Father has for us. Another way of saying this is to say that there begins to be formed within us something of a shepherd's heart which is deeply moved by humans and human waywardness. Please notice that "heart of a shepherd" means being able to look at wolves in their sheepliness. It is not a question of us fearing that there are many people dressed as sheep who are, in fact, wolves, but, on the contrary, of being able *creatively* to imagine wolves, in some more or less well hidden part of their lives, as in fact sheep, and to love them as such. Various times in the Gospel the word *splangchnidzomai* crops up, which we usually translate as "moved with compassion." Jesus was moved with compassion by this or that person or situation or because the multitudes should be like sheep having no shepherd (Matt. 9:36). However the word is rather strong and means a deep commotion of the entrails, a visceral commotion. This is what is so hard to imagine: as we become unhooked from our partisan loves, our searches, our clinging to reputation, with these formed in reaction to this situation or that, there begins to be formed in us that absolutely gratuitous visceral commotion, born outside all reaction, which the ancients called *agapé* and which is nothing other than the inexplicable love which God has for us in our violence and our scandals. We begin to be able not only to know ourselves loved as human beings, but to be able to love other humans, to love the human race and condition.

It seems to me that here we have something of the reason that the Church has always conceived the saints in glory as in some way helping us by their intercession and their miracles: you could not be a saint and not have an inexplicable visceral commotion toward humanity, in imitation of the self-giving visceral commotion of Jesus, who, let us remember:

---

4. I am thinking here of the sort of sympathy that some who are kidnapped come to feel for their kidnappers, known as "The Stockholm Syndrome." It is not this that Luke is portraying.

...for the joy that was set before him endured the cross, thought nothing of the shame, and is seated at God's right hand.

(Heb. 12:2)

The joy in question was not merely the promise of an eschatological vindication, nor a fixation on what was to be Jesus' own fruition when all the trials were over, but it was the possibility of delighting forever in a huge celebration along with a huge multitude of us human beings, people who are good, bad, creative, depressive, but humans and, for that reason, loved. Something of that appears to have been understood by that most English of martyrs, St. Thomas More, who, as a former Chancellor of the Realm, understood very well his complicity in the order of this world, when he expressed the desire, as the prospect of the block loomed closer, that he and his executioner should "be jocund together at the heavenly banquet." Not merely the indispensable forgiving of his persecutor, but an inexplicable delight in his sister humanity.

Images that Run Together

Throughout these pages there have been two imaginative poles, two principal images, which have given us hints for the understanding of something of the things that are above on which we are to fix our minds: the vision of the open heaven with the risen victim — the slaughtered lamb standing or seated at the right hand of God — and the wedding banquet. In fact these two images permeate the whole apostolic witness: shortly after John the Baptist points Jesus out as the lamb of God and shortly after Nathanael is promised that he will see the heavens opened and the angels of God ascending and descending upon the Son of man, Jesus works his first sign, in Cana of Galilee. The sign is that the bridegroom of Israel has arrived and the one who was an abandoned and repudiated[5] woman is beginning to be able to enjoy a wedding banquet where flow a wine and a rejoicing quite unthinkably greater than that imagined by those who had made the wedding preparations. I do not need to mention the number of times that Jesus speaks of the kingdom in terms of a wed-

---

5. Cf. Isaiah 62:1–5; that this interpretation is according to the mind of the Church can be seen by looking at the readings for the second Sunday of the year in cycle C, where the Isaiah passage and the wedding at Cana are juxtaposed.

ding banquet in the synoptic Gospels, for we have looked at several of those passages.

What is indeed interesting is the running together of these images in the book of Revelation, the book where all is centered around the heavenly vision of the slaughtered lamb. Let us look at the passage:

> And I heard as it were the voice of a great multitude, and as the voice of many waters, and as the voice of mighty thunderings, saying, Alleluia: for the Lord our God, the omnipotent, has begun to reign! Let us rejoice and leap for joy and give God the glory! For the marriage of the Lamb has come, and his bride is made ready for him, it has been given her to dress in resplendent pure linen (and the linen is the works of justice of the saints). Then [the angel] said to me: "Write: blessed are those who are invited to the wedding banquet of the lamb." And he said, "These are true words of God." (Rev. 19:6–9)

The two images flow into one alone: the wedding banquet of the lamb. And this confluence of images has as its effect precisely that we should learn to imagine the things that are above, that we should allow ourselves to be nurtured by this imagination which will empower us to re-create that wedding banquet. On the one hand we have the gratuity of the invitation made to good and bad alike, allowing us to stand loose from concern about how appropriate our participation might be, because the invitation, and it is insistent, comes from One who delights in us just as we are. On the other hand this same standing loose, this same unconcern, gets through to us in the degree to which we allow ourselves to be possessed by the news that God is entirely without violence, is utterly vivacious, creative, effervescent, that we are empowered for the construction of a story of life in flexible imitation of the risen victim. This is a story which we construct in hope, and by which we construct hope, creating belief, in the midst of the crushing darkness of the dominion of death. That is, the apostolic witness itself shows clearly that the inner dynamic which runs through it reaches maturity precisely in this fusion of images which come together to form a single vision of heaven.

But there is more: the banquet is not only a banquet, but it is a wedding banquet, and the guests also constitute the bride. That is, the rejoicing is not only that of guests, but of one being married, and here is where the image of heaven is, without any shame, marital. The wedding which is celebrated includes the completely loving interpenetration of bride and groom, in a relationship which makes of them one thing, a relation of infinitely creative fecundity, freed, of course, from all the tensions, rivalries, and complications which surround and diminish our experience and living out of things erotic. Paul points this out when he explains marriage in Ephesians 5, comparing the conjugal relationship to that between Christ and the Church, but please notice that he doesn't start from the conjugal relationship in order to explain heaven, but it is the heavenly relationship, that of heavenly self-giving and interpenetration in love, which is his starting point for understanding the earthly reality of marriage. It seems to me that this image is also to nourish our hope-fired imaginations: it is the story of the ugly duckling, of Cinderella, made, much to her surprise, capable and worthy of a relationship of loving exchange with her swan, her prince, quite beyond her expectations. When Paul says that, at the end, everything will be subdued to Christ, who will be submitted to God, "so that God may be all in all" (1 Cor. 15:28), it is to be understood within this interpenetrative vision. Since we are formed from within entirely by the Other who has called us into existence, since "the other is consubstantial with the consciousness of the 'self,' "[6] at the end we will be entirely possessed by the God who possesses pacifically in an interchange that is ever more fecund and creative. We will be married participants, all our desires fulfilled, in that effervescent creative vitality.

The Nourished Imagination and the Re-creation of Desire

We could leave the matter there, but I think that something would be missing in our attempt to recover the eschatological imagination which characterizes the apostolic witness. This business of fixing the mind on the things that are above might be understood to be merely a cerebral exercise, a matter of thinking. I'm far from wanting to undervalue the importance of a certain intellectual rigor when thinking about such things, but it is certainly not enough. Something is missing from our recovery of the eschatological imagination, and it is the dimension of praise, that is, of glorifying God. Here I move with some care, for a banalization of praise has taken place, whereby some in the Church seem to imagine that it is only a matter of say-

---

6. J.-M. Oughourlian, *Un mime nommé désir* (Paris: Grasset, 1982), 58.

ing "Glory to God" in a loud, insistent, and public manner, while on the other hand there has been a loss of the authentic liturgical sense of the "Gloria" and the "Sanctus" in so many of our Masses, the sense of reverent participation in a heavenly liturgy around the human victim even now in glory, rather than in a self-celebration of the community.

We have already seen that glorifying God means giving God the reputation which is really appropriate, causing God's name to have a good reputation on earth, as it does in heaven, and that this means giving a good reputation to human victims, to that which is not. I think that this is the basis of the insistence of many passages from the apostolic texts that it is *in the midst of trials and tribulations* that we are to rejoice and to praise God. For it is in the midst of trials, being on the way out of being, where we are, in fact, giving a just reputation to God. Let us look, for example, at Luke 6:22–23:

> Blessed are you when they hate you and drive you out and insult you and utter all sorts of calumnies against you on account of the Son of man. Rejoice in that day and jump for joy, for great will be your reward in heaven, for it was thus that their fathers treated the prophets.

The whole of chapter 8 of the epistle to the Romans is an act of praise of the God who frees us from being scandalized by ourselves (cf. Rom. 7:18–8:2); and it is the Spirit which pleads on our behalf with sighs too deep for words while we are sharing the sufferings of Jesus which enables Paul to say

> ...that the sufferings of this present time are as nothing compared with the glory which will one day be revealed in us.
>
> (Rom. 8:18)

Now I'd like to point out that this insistence on our rejoicing (cf. Phil. 4:4–6), singing, and praising God, is *not* in the first place because God is short of praise, for there are myriad angels and saints caught up in this. Rather, as the Common Preface IV of the Roman Missal has it:

> You have no need of our praise, but our desire to give you thanks is itself your gift. Our thanksgiving adds nothing to your greatness, but makes us grow in your grace....

That is, the principal reason for this insistence on rejoicing, on praising, on singing, is that it helps us come out of ourselves and to open out our imaginations so that we may be nourished by that infinite effervescence and generosity of which we have spoken.

It is here, I think, that the treatise on angels has its place. By angels I understand beings created by God in such a way that each one is a different genus. It is not as though there were a genus "angels," as there is the genus "birds," and then a division into different species — water birds, birds of prey, and so on. Each angel is a different genus, something completely without parallel. It seems to me that the whole sense of this traditional insistence is to oblige us to stretch our imaginations toward something of the extraordinary and unimagined diversity of beauties, of forms, of ways of being, which are completely beyond us. The underlying idea is that these creatures of God remind us of that which we cannot imagine directly at all: God's absolutely creative vitality and over-brimming, for whom creating unsuspected and breathlessly daring novelties continuously and dynamically is a mere nothing.

And we are not invited to imagine these things that are above as part of a game. Rather it is precisely at the times of darkness, of being crushed, of shadows, that they take on their greatest importance. It seems to me not at all surprising that Jesus should have taught his disciples that they should neither despise the little ones, nor cause them to stumble, in terms of angels:

> Take heed that ye despise not one of these little ones; for I say unto you, that in heaven their angels do always behold the face of my Father which is in heaven. (Matt. 18:10)

To a situation of being despised here there corresponds an opening of the imagination that begins to understand a beauty and a worth "there" which is not yet understood "below."

The angels appear at Jesus' birth in the same guise: during a census in which the whole world had to go and give its details, a child is born in an insignificant place, and an innumerable multitude of the heavenly host appear, giving glory to God, to certain poor shepherds, the people considered at that time most base, despicable, and likely to steal (cf. Luke 2:8–20). The fact that the angels were innumerable is important, for it shows up the complete futility of the census, which wanted to count people, but which would have no idea how to contemplate either the importance of the newborn child, nor the sheer quantity of glorious celestial accompaniment that came with him. To straitened circumstances here, there corresponds an amplitude of glory in heaven.

Perhaps the most important glimpse we get of this principle at work is in Jesus' arrest, in Matthew's version. In that straitened circumstance, one of Jesus' companions takes out a sword and cuts off the ear of the high priest's servant. Jesus says to him:

> Put your sword back into its place, for those who take up the sword shall die by the sword. Or do you think that I cannot pray to my Father, and he will straightway place beside me more than twelve legions of angels? But then, how would the Scriptures be fulfilled which say that thus must it come to pass?
> (Matt. 26:52–54)

We can see it very clearly: at a time of persecution, the old earthly imagination thinks immediately of armed reciprocity, and Jesus stops it with a phrase which demonstrates exactly that he is condemning that imagination, which only serves the reciprocal increase of the kingdom of death. His imagination *in the midst of this straitened circumstance* is fixed on his Father, on his glorious vitality and splendorous power in so many angels, in such a way that he doesn't need to act out of reciprocity, out of imitative rivalry. Rather it is this very imagination which is empowering him to carry out that for which he came, his loving self-giving into the hands of violent men, the fulfillment of the Scriptures.

So the presence of the angels forms part of an insistence that we praise God and open our imagination, allowing it to rest on so much creativity, splendor, and beauty. This is especially important when we are in situations of persecution, turbulence, or anguish, where there seems to be no way out. It is there, where there are no open doors, that we have to fix on the open heaven, the humble and unappetizing door of the victim, and on the multitude of angels, signs of God's creative effervescence. True praise and glorification of God pass "upward" not through a big gate, but through something much closer to the eye of the needle of which Jesus also spoke to indicate that what is impossible for us is not impossible for God. The imagination of God's possibilities, of what God is able to do in the midst of the impossibilities of the world, always passes through a very narrow fissure. However the praise and glorification of God does not merely function as a way of nourishing our imagination when all seems lost, but it has an even more important rôle. Learning to imagine the things that are above, to come out of ourselves in praise, also serves to create within us a new desire. If we are unable to imagine heaven, neither are we able to long for it.

Here it seems to me that we have a key issue: the revelation of God's absolutely creative vitality serves to re-create and nourish our imagination, and, at the same time, the fact that we be induced into praising God, opening out our imagination, works to allow us to be seduced by the beauty and joy that alone serve to re-create in us ever deeper desires which will never be frustrated, which will be satisfied and fulfilled beyond our wildest hopes. It is not for nothing that an Elder points the seer of Revelation to those who are dressed in white, bringing together elements from Isaiah (Isa. 49:10 and 25:8) and from Psalm 23, mixing them with the image of the lamb standing slain in the center of the heavenly liturgy:

> These are they which have come out of the great tribulation, and have washed their robes and made them white in the blood of the lamb. It is because of this that they are before the throne of God, and serve him day and night in his temple: and he that sitteth on the throne shall dwell among them. They shall hunger no more, neither thirst any more; neither shall they suffer the scorching of the sun, *for the lamb which is in the midst of the throne shall feed them, and shall lead them unto living fountains of waters: and God shall wipe away all tears from their eyes.* (Rev. 7:14–17, emphasis added)

Fountains of living water! The biblical symbol *par excellence,* proper to a harsh, dry Middle Eastern land, of human desire absolutely fulfilled, without frustration, running over, harmonious and peaceable. It is this same fountain which Jesus had offered to the woman at the well of Samaria, instead of the water which does not satisfy:

> The one who drinks of the water which I shall give will never more be thirsty: for the water that I shall give will become in that person a spring of water welling up into life without end.
> (John 4:14)

The fixing of the mind on the things that are above has as its end to re-create in us a pacific imitative desire which does not know frustration, but whose longing, viscerally moved, is to participate actively, by creating the wedding banquet of the lamb in the midst of this world, in God's creative vivaciousness, utterly incapable of frustration.

Conclusion

There is, I find, a passage from the apostolic witness which is a kind of resumé of everything I have been seeking to say in these pages. And what is so extraordinary is that everything, absolutely everything, is there, insinuated by means of different images, of course, but, beyond any shadow of doubt, there. So we could say that this whole book is but a long gloss on that passage. You will find present the apocalyptic imagination as something past; its vision of God who causes trembling, also past; the world of the violent sacred, which has been overcome; and in their stead a new vision, the eschatological vision, centered on the living vitality of God which is emphasized by angels, mediated by the blood of the lamb. The passage even hints that this vision is to be understood as the definitive bringing to an end of the world order which was born with Cain, the order of the world since the first victim. And this vision is offered to those who hear as a means of nurturing their imagination so that they may live with boldness the hope opened up by Jesus. We will allow the author of the epistle to the Hebrews to speak for himself:

> For you have not come unto what can be touched[7] and to a burning fire, nor unto dense clouds and tempest, nor unto the sound of a trumpet and the clamor of words, which were such that those who heard beseeched that they should not be spoken any more. For they could not endure what was commanded, "Whosoever shall touch the mountain, even if it be a beast, shall be stoned to death." So terrible was the spectacle that Moses said, "I fear exceedingly and I quake." Instead you have come to Mount Zion, to the city of the living God, the heavenly Jerusalem; to the myriad angels, to the gathering together of the first born who are inscribed in heaven; to God, judge of all and the spirits of the just who have arrived at their goal; to the mediator of a new covenant, Jesus, and to the blood of aspersion which speaks more strongly than the blood of Abel. (Heb. 12:18–24)

---

7. Some ancient texts read *orei*, a *mount* that can be touched, referring to Sinai.

It behooves us, then, with this last shake to the imagination, as well as those that have gone before, to make of our lives the joyous preparation of the feast of the innocent victim.

•

A small conclusive note. The Lord tells us quite specifically not to cast our pearls before swine (Matt. 7:6). Yet, and in marked contrast with his own injunction, whenever he gives some would-be theologian a little spark of heavenly vision, asking that person to make of it something with which to feed his sheep, the Lord is in fact casting his pearl before a swine. I fear that the too evident discrepancy between the pearl and the swine who interprets it may be a cause of stumbling (cf. Matt. 23:3). So I ask the Lord to allow you to distinguish well, and without scandal between pearl and swine, and I ask you to pray that the swine may be made ever more adequate to the pearl, instead of further muddying it with his swinery, even though, when all is said and done, swine are humans too!

Index